SEEKING THE WAY

SEEKING THE WAY

A CHRISTIAN'S GUIDE TO
INNER PEACE AND FULFILLMENT

TIM CRAIN

© 2015 Tim Crain. All rights reserved. No part of this document may be reproduced or transmitted in any form or by any means, electronic or mechanical, including photocopying, recording, or by an information storage and retrieval system – except by a reviewer who may quote brief passages in a review to be printed in a magazine, newspaper, or on the Web – without permission in writing from the author.

Although the author and publisher have made every effort to ensure the accuracy and completeness of information contained in this book, we assume no responsibility for errors, inaccuracies, omissions, or any inconsistency herein. Any slights of people, places, or organizations are unintentional.

Cover Design by Brian Halley
Layout Design by Nikki Ward, Morrison Alley Design

First Printing 2015

ISBN 978-0-9960788-3-2

This book is dedicated to my loving wife and children. I pray God's love and peace will be with you for all the days of your lives.

Table of Contents

Introduction		i
Chapter 1	Seeking The Way	1
Chapter 2	Living in God's Light	20
Chapter 3	Faith and Inner Peace	40
Chapter 4	Foundations of a Fulfilling Life	69
Chapter 5	Your Values and Purpose	96
Chapter 6	Temptations and Distractions	117
Chapter 7	Relationships and Support	140
Chapter 8	Finding the Way	162
Conclusion	Walking the Path	184
Questions	Questions to Help You Seek the Way	187
About the Author		195

Introduction

> *Turn from evil and do good; seek peace and pursue it.*
> — Psalm 34:14

Faith leads to peace. Trust in God, and he will calm your mind and your spirit.

That's a message all of us have heard many times over, but do we actually believe it? And if it's true, why do so many believers struggle with anxiety over the direction of their lives, making major decisions, and a feeling of being unfulfilled?

It is true, of course, but the reality of worldly life is that things aren't so simple. Faith *does* bring peace, but it's not as simple as saying a few words and watching all of your worries vanish into thin air. Like a lot of things involving Christianity, the principles of contentment are relatively straightforward, but living within them isn't necessarily so.

It doesn't just take a belief in God to find his path for you, but also a commitment to understanding Scripture, openness to his plan for your life, and a continual commitment to renewing that faith.

That's what *Seeking the Way* is all about. By using biblical lessons as a map to life's journey, we can not only understand what God wants from us in our lives, but also go through each day with a clearer idea of what we can do to find the happiness and contentment he has to offer.

There isn't anyone I can think of who couldn't benefit from a greater level of calm, happiness, and contentment. If you feel that your life is lacking one or more of those things right now, the ideas you'll find in the coming pages can help you move closer to a path that feels fulfilling to you. If you're already in a great place with your faith, and the direction of your life, the following chapters will help you understand why – and just as important, what you can do to avoid being pulled away into strife and confusion.

There are a lot of books out there on biblical living, and even more of them on the general concept of happiness. What makes this title different is the combination of Scripture, self-discovery, and examination. If you're reading this, I probably don't know you personally; and even if I did, I wouldn't know you well enough to be able to tell you what kinds of things are in your heart and what kinds of changes you need to make in your life.

God knows those things, though, and will help you learn them about yourself if you aren't sure. What *Seeking the Way* does is give you a personal roadmap you can follow to faith, happiness, and contentment again and again – even as your life, goals, and circumstances change.

Regardless of what people might tell you, there isn't a "one-size-fits-all" approach to finding the perfect life.

That's true even among believers. Because God gives us all different talents, gifts, and wishes, it shouldn't be surprising that he gives us all different paths to follow, as well.

The more you can know about *your* path, and the more you can structure your life in a way that's aligned with it, the more joy you're going to feel. Believers have known that for centuries, and I'm certainly not the first author to point it out. But I can give you a set of tips and ideas that pull you closer to your true purpose and help you thrive – emotionally, spiritually, and otherwise – in our uncertain modern world.

All lives have ups and downs. Yours will, too, regardless of whether or not you read this book and follow along in the pages and activities that are still to come. But the happiest and most productive people combine their faith and belief with a sense of purpose that doesn't just drive them forward, but also gives them the inner peace that all people crave. In other words, you can't stop bad or unexpected things from happening, but you can control how you manage them and the effect they have on your life.

The Lord wants us to be happy and loved, which is why he gave us each other, along with good life advice to follow within the different books of the Bible. Let's take a look at some of the key ideas and verses together, so you can see what happens when you decide to start *Seeking the Way*...

CHAPTER ONE

Seeking The Way

Peace I leave with you; my peace I give you. I do not give to you as the world gives. Do not let your hearts be troubled and do not be afraid.

— John 14:27

*I*f God and his word are the way to wisdom, peace, and contentment, why do they seem so elusive sometimes? This is a question almost every one of the 2 billion+ Christians on the planet have asked themselves at some point or another. Do we lack the faith we need, or are we misinterpreting the teachings of Jesus? And how can we organize our lives – and ourselves – in a way that brings us back into his light?

I won't pretend there are easy answers to those questions. Even though some level of struggle and conflict is bound to be present in our life here on earth, I don't think these doubts and troubles are impossible to overcome. In fact, my own research and experience has led me to a set of habits and philosophies we can use to reignite ourselves and live with the love and peace God wants for us.

I've distilled them into this book, *Seeking the Way*, in the hopes that you can use them to feel closer to Christ and his salvation in your own life.

A Tale of Two Believers

I want you to stop for a minute and imagine two believers, Bob and John, sitting beside each other on a church pew somewhere. It doesn't matter where they come from or how old they are. What's important about them are respective moods and mindsets that are shaping their thoughts, their actions, and even their futures.

Bob is calm and at ease. His life seems to be going pretty well, albeit with the ups and downs here and there that we all experience. He wakes up every morning feeling refreshed and goes to bed at night feeling comforted and at peace. He faces the same kinds of temptations we all do in our day-to-day lives, but he's mostly able to shrug them off and keep his focus on what really matters to him over the long term, not the things that seem flashy or pressing in the moment. Bob feels strong in his faith and convictions, but more than that, he feels secure in himself.

Because of this mixture of confidence, purpose, and compassion, he is able to enjoy every moment more fully and build deeper relationships with others. He trusts people, and they trust him back, in a way that shows. Even the biggest stumbling blocks in life don't shake him in his beliefs or path. Bob knows what he's on this earth to do and feels happy and content with the part he is playing.

As a believer, John has the same *faith* but none of the *fulfillment*. He constantly wonders whether he's on the right path, if he'll be able to resist his sharpest temptations, and whether he's really living out a plan God had for him. He feels nervous and untrusting, sometimes wondering if even his closest relationships are authentic.

John is constantly bouncing from one idea or notion to the other, looking for a "quick fix" to a particularly difficult problem. He wants his faith to be secure, but it feels like he's being tried and tested constantly. The turmoil is slowly but surely spilling over to a lot of different parts of his life, with disastrous effects to his health, career, and marriage.

There are obviously a lot of contrasts between these two fictional individuals, but the reality is most of us fluctuate between one extreme and another for most of our lives. At some points, we feel happy and content, like Bob. We get the sense that God has a plan for us and it's working out. Other times, we feel shaken, scared, or even defeated, as John does. We're thrown off the path and start to wonder whether we'll ever find it again – or if it ever existed at all.

As you've probably figured out by now, *Seeking the Way* is all about moving yourself to that first category. It's not just about finding your peace but holding on to it, even in the toughest of times. It's about living the life you are meant to have in a way that pleases God and lets him share his earthly gifts with us.

Living in God's Light

Throughout this book, you'll find me using the terms "on the path" or "in the light" somewhat interchangeably. The truth is, it doesn't really matter what term you use to describe being at peace in your life and walking the path God has for us. What *is* important is the recognition that it's something all of us are striving for.

When we are on the path, things just seem to be happening with their own momentum. Our faith is strong, of course, but things just seem to "click." Our work is fulfilling, our relationships are healthy, and we even find ourselves enjoying the gifts and talents God has given us more.

Obviously, this has to do with the sense of peace I've already brought up, but it's about more than simply feeling content. It's also about being energized, engaged, and even excited – you aren't just happy about the way life is going, but you're looking forward to what comes next, too.

Most of us have experienced this wonderful state from time to time, but we may have mistakenly thought it was little more than a good mood, or a "nice patch of luck."

While that can be the case sometimes, and there are certain trials and tribulations that make it difficult to feel like you're in the light, that doesn't mean finding it has to be rare, or an accident.

To stay on the path, we have to set the right conditions for peace, fulfillment, and excitement while living in accordance with a handful of biblical principles (the ones we'll walk through in the remaining chapters).

Given that living in the light feels so wonderful, why don't more Christians make an effort to experience it more often? From my perspective, it really comes down to a few common misconceptions…

Isn't Faith Enough?

It has been said many times, by many people, that a bit of faith in the Lord is all that's truly needed for a happy life. Learn to trust him and accept that his will is going to eventually be done, even if it doesn't coincide with your immediate desires, and you'll be just fine.

I think that notion is half-correct. Having a strong sense of faith and belief can keep you grounded and allow you to weather almost any storm. It helps you to hold on to the right perspective in your life and roots you in something much, much stronger than yourself.

And yet, we see every day that having faith isn't enough to prevent mental, emotional, and even spiritual upheaval.

There are tens of millions of Christians walking around, right this very second, with anguish that seems literally overwhelming. Why don't more of them find the peace they're crying out for?

In my own experience, one reason is that some people *expect* a certain degree of pain and difficulty and will tend to look for it wherever they can. They know this world is imperfect and have an almost prophetical desire to be tested so they can show just how strong their faith and resolve actually are. In other words, they look forward to hardship – or at least expect it – and will generate it if they can't find it in their own lives.

While there is some biblical precedent to the idea of believers being tested for their faith, I don't personally believe that our God wants us to live in perpetual fear and struggle. If he did, why leave so many references to the peace of spirit that we should all be seeking?

Here are a few of my favorites:

Submit to God and be at peace with him; in this way prosperity will come to you.
– Job 22:21

The Lord gives strength to his people; the Lord blesses his people with peace.
– Psalm 29:11

Glory to God in the highest heaven, and on earth peace to those on whom his favor rests.

— Luke 2:14

Struggle is a part of our earthly lives, but that doesn't mean it has to be a constant feature of our day-to-day existence. If anything, I think God gives us our faith to ease our burden, not add to it.

Dealing With Day-to-Day Struggles

Some Christians, and especially newer ones, seem to have the opposite problem. The first few months or years of their faith are like a honeymoon. They essentially fall in love with God and the idea of his everlasting love. That's not a bad thing, of course, but it can leave you with the notion that everything should be easy and blissful. That's just not the way life on earth works.

No matter how strong your faith is, and how excited you are about your beliefs, there are going to be roadblocks that fall in your way. You're still going to get sick, have to worry about your finances, lose people you love, and otherwise deal with the same problems that the rest of humanity does. Expecting them all to fall away just because you've accepted Jesus isn't just unrealistic; it's setting yourself up for disappointment later.

As a matter of fact, Jesus actually told us directly that we should expect to have troubles in this world. It's important for us to accept this is true and not anticipate a life that's free from struggle. Once we acknowledge that the road won't always be easy, we can begin to look for his peace and his guiding hand in our lives. The Lord has already warned us that our journey won't be without its struggles, but he has also assured us that we can find peace through him.

Just as the Bible never says that your life has to be filled with constant toil and anguish, neither does it promise that every difficulty is going to evaporate the minute you open your heart to God. Trust me, if it did, you would have heard about it by now.

What we're really talking about in both cases are misplaced expectations. If you expect life to be filled with pain and disappointment, that's all you're going to see in this world. You'll be too closed off to all the wonderful joys of being human to enjoy them. And on the other hand, if you take it for granted that everything is going to come easily for you without any effort simply because you've taken God's word to heart, you're missing the point.

Peace and uninterrupted happiness aren't always the same thing. Uninterrupted happiness is an illusion, because all earthly things that bring us joy and elation are fleeting.

The world tells us to seek out high engagement and excitement. It tells us to crave a life that's "on the edge," where we always feel like our favorite sports team just won the championship or we have won the lottery. These occurrences are almost always rare, however, and the happiness we get from them doesn't last.

To understand how that must always be the case, think back to the last time you had a birthday party or a very nice dinner out. As great as those experiences were, did they permanently change your mood or the sense of satisfaction you have with your life? Of course not. None of the things the world gives us can provide real contentment.

Peace, on the other hand, stays with you even when you aren't feeling happy. It's not so much a temporary feeling as it is a state of being. Happiness is great, but you should never expect momentary excitement to last for long. Instead, strive for the kind of faith and inner peace that will live inside of you forever.

Being Pushed From Your Path

I should point out here that there are also Christians who are struggling to find peace and comfort, at least temporarily. These are men and women who have suffered extreme shocks in life, such as a serious illness or the loss of a loved one. Regardless of how close you are to God's path in your life, some unexpected events feel like a strong wind pushing you off to one side and into the weeds of chaos.

I know this because I've seen it time and time again. I've even lived it.

Several years ago, I relocated my family to pursue a new career opportunity. The change was exciting, and everything felt new and fresh. Then, within a year, the financial crisis that was shaking the country affected my business. Suddenly, it wasn't just my job and income that were potentially in jeopardy, but also the wisdom of my past decisions.

Being in the financial industry, my business was at the forefront of the crisis. I had taken my wife and children away from their friends, and plunged their lives into turmoil, to do what I had thought was right at the time. But in the face of a downturn that looked like it could descend into a full-blown economic depression, I was contemplating what steps I might have to take if things got worse.

As the leader of my family and our provider, I felt as if a rug had been pulled out from beneath my feet. What had seemed like such a promising career move might have been slipping away right in front of me.

At that time, when things seemed to be at their darkest, I did the best thing I knew how to: I put my faith in God, prayed for his guidance, and kept working as hard as I could. In time, things smoothed out in the financial industry and my worries about the direction of my career faded away.

But the lesson I took from that event wasn't that the market is cyclical, but that the Lord is ready to step in and give you calm if you're only willing to trust his plan. I couldn't control what was happening around me – or even what would happen *to* me – but I could use my faith to ease the burden. That's important for all of us to remember when it matters most.

A Few Notes on This Book...

This book isn't like most of the other books you'll ever read, and for that reason there are a few things I should probably explain or introduce before we get down to business. After all, I'm hoping what you'll read – and more important, what you'll do – in the coming chapters will literally change your life for the better.

In order for that to happen, however, I need you to trust me, follow along, and participate. So it makes sense that I should start out with who I actually am, and how I came up with these ideas, so you can have a little faith in me as we go along.

The name you see on the cover, Tim Crain, might not mean a lot to you. I'm not the pastor of a mega church (or even a small one), a renowned religious scholar, or even a household name. Who I am is a fellow believer with a curious mind and a habit of looking at things like faith, spirituality, and fulfillment a little bit differently than the rest of the world.

Know that what you're about to read works because I've lived it, researched it, and seen it transform lives for other people again and again. This isn't merely a set of ideas; it's my life's work, arrived at through decades of thought and reflection.

When I first came across these concepts, I was concerned with one of the biggest and most important (but often unanswered) questions in life: Why do so many people find it hard to define the success they want for themselves, much less achieve it? I had seen time and time again how material wealth and high-profile achievements left people feeling empty and searching for more. In the process of finding the answers, I found a very strong and persistent link between faith, peace, and engagement.

The resulting insights led to the release of my first book, *Seeking Your Center*. In it, I look at the failure of things like wealth and job status to feel satisfying in a (mostly) secular way. I introduce faith as an important ingredient to getting the most out of life, but intentionally left the door open for those who are still exploring their beliefs to seek out answers on their own.

We are all on different points along life's path. As such, we are also individually trying to process, analyze, and achieve happiness on our respective journeys. It cannot be emphasized enough that each of these journeys is unique.

They are so unique, in fact, that no one has ever walked your path or mine throughout all of history. And for all of eternity, no one will ever walk these paths again. Due to the uniqueness of these journeys, I want to provide guidance and support to all, regardless of where they might be mentally or spiritually in a particular moment.

For me, *Seeking Your Center* is a very helpful guide to those trying to find the inner peace they want in their lives. I always knew I wanted to pursue the idea even further within my own faith, with the goal of offering another version that would speak directly to Christians.

In that way, you can think of the book you're holding in your hands (or maybe viewing on your screen) as a companion to *Seeking Your Center*, a more faith-based alternative, or just the next natural step from where it leaves off. Really, it's all of those things at the same time. You don't have to read *Seeking Your Center* to understand or appreciate the lessons and activities in this book, but it won't be a problem for you if you've already gone through it, either – there is some overlap between them, although you'll obviously get more of a faith-based approach here.

Speaking of faith, it's also important for me to point out that the ideas you'll find in the coming chapters come from the Bible. In many places you'll find that I've quoted Scripture directly, with the footprint of God's word lingering in other sections.

Knowing that, it might be reasonable for you to ask yourself whether you even need to read this book. After all, aren't all the answers there in the Bible? In my experience, they are, and this book certainly isn't intended to replace regular Bible study. But you may find that the ideas and exercises within will enhance it.

Let me explain: Like a lot of people I know, I can get a great deal from reading a bit of Scripture each day. What I *can't* do, though, is memorize lots of chapter-and-verse references like some others can. My mind just doesn't work that way. And even if I could, finding the verses I'm looking for on a daily or weekly basis would be difficult, even if I highlighted and bookmarked them repeatedly (something I've done in the past).

Throughout this book, you'll find references to different bits of Scripture (specifically, from the NIV version I prefer). Some are directly relevant to the topic, while others are just personal favorites. What I want you to remember at each stage is that my goal is to help you summarize and organize some of the biblical thoughts about peace, contentment, passion, and purpose in your life. It's God's word that's serving as the inspiration here, not my opinions about your life. I've tried to stay true to his message as clearly and cleanly as possible.

That's not to say I have all the answers, though. While I've developed the material for this book over the course of a lifetime, it's my interpretation of God's word, based on a biblical foundation. As the old saying goes, "Your mileage may vary."

The material you're reading in this book has been proven to be effective for a lot of different people, myself included, over a significant frame of time. It's not just based on my own life, but also on the experiences of godly, successful people. It's one thing to disagree with me; it's another to say that former presidents, and leaders like Rev. Dr. Martin Luther King Jr., had it all wrong, too.

What they knew, and what I've discovered in my own life, is that there *is* a formula for living in God's light, if you're willing to find it and work at it on a daily basis. In fact, many of its pieces even work for people who either aren't Christians or wouldn't consider themselves regular churchgoers and Scripture-readers.

Still, as you read these pages, I'm going to make a couple of assumptions about you. First, I'm going to assume that you're either a believer or someone who is at least open to allowing Christ in your life. If this doesn't sound like you, or if you disagree with that viewpoint, feel free to put this book down now and pick up a copy of *Seeking Your Center*.

Note that I'm *not* advocating for any particular church or denomination (either mine or yours), because I think that within the context of this book the separations aren't that important. If you believe Jesus is important to your life and want to have a better relationship with him, yourself, and everyone else around you, we can agree on the major points in that matter.

With that out of the way, let's get to the other assumption I'm making about you: that you wish you could enjoy a little more peace in your life, or at least feel it more regularly. If you recognize yourself in that statement, know that you aren't alone and that there is an answer. Finding it is what *Seeking the Way* is all about.

How to Get the Most From Seeking the Way

I've already mentioned this book isn't like other books because of the huge impact I think it can have on your life. There's another important way that it's different, too: In order for it to make a difference, you have to participate yourself.

Although I'm going to be sharing a bit of Scripture, and the odd personal story, the real answers to be found aren't in my words, but your insights. Every one of us is different, something I'll come back to again later, meaning the answers that work for me won't necessarily be the right ones for you, and vice versa.

Don't worry; that doesn't mean you're going to be pushing forward on your own. At each step in the process, I'm going to introduce some important concepts and principles that apply to all of us. It's going to be up to you, though, to figure out how they relate to you specifically.

One easy, helpful, and time-tested way to do that is by using a journal. You may have noticed that there is an accompanying workbook you can purchase along with *Seeking the Way*. Using one, and filling in the pages as you go, can help you save time and organize your thoughts. It's certainly not required, however, and a regular notebook or legal pad will do just as well.

Regardless of how you're taking notes, try to get into the habit of writing regularly and extensively. That is, I want you to put your pen to paper every day, if possible, for at least 20 or 30 minutes of time. Let your mind roam free. Don't stop exploring a question or topic until you feel like you've emptied your mind on the subject, and don't be afraid to come back and add more material again later. It may not be easy, but it is the most important thing you can do to find the kind of peace and excitement you're looking for.

You may also find that a little bit of daily meditation or reflection helps you think through the issues more clearly. The topics we're going to be covering are big ones, concerning the strength of your faith, the depth of your beliefs, and your true purpose in life. Don't expect to find a quick resolution or inspiration coming to you off the top of your head. The simple nature of day-to-day life on earth is that most of us push these thoughts down, consciously or unconsciously, so we can think about other things. They won't necessarily rise back to the surface easily, or without help.

And finally, know that the human condition is one of constant motion and change. That's a nice way of saying God's path for you doesn't run in a straight line, nor is it without its jagged rocks and weeds, and your understanding of it is likely to shift over time – don't hope for an easy path, but expect a challenging one. The most fulfilled and successful people I know go through some version of these exercises on a regular basis. Many of them are surprised to find their answers and priorities move without having them ever notice. The farther you feel from the path, the more likely it is you need to do some reading, journaling, and reflecting before you can find the way back again.

Are You Ready to Step Into the Light?

There's an old saying that "nothing worth doing is easy to do," and I find that to generally be true. The harder you work at something, the bigger reward you'll usually find waiting for you at the end.

This is a good time to mention that just because the road ahead isn't complicated, that doesn't mean it's easy, either. There are probably going to be times when you'll be tempted to give up on a question, skip over a chapter, or look for the answers that seem easiest so you can move on.

Don't fall for the temptation.

It's always more convenient to settle for the life you have, or to simply give up on the idea of finding peace, contentment, and an extra sense of passion in your life. But all of those things are there for you to achieve, if only you're willing to stand up and do a little bit of work to get them.

You're about to take the first steps on one of the most important journeys of your life. Let's learn more about *Seeking the Way* and discovering God's plan for you…

SEEKING THE WAY

✓ *When have you felt most at peace in your life?*

✓ *Can you list two times when you were able to see God working in your life?*

✓ *What are the biggest areas in your life right now where you need to show more trust in God?*

CHAPTER TWO

Living in God's Light

Cast your cares on the Lord and he will sustain you; he will never let the righteous be shaken.

– Psalm 55:22

In the opening of this book, I talked briefly about living "in God's light" and "on the path," trying to describe that wonderful feeling we all crave. But, given that no one – regardless of how strong their faith is – is going to feel that sense of peace all the time, does it still make sense to follow the steps in *Seeking the Way*?

I absolutely think so. Not only will being on the path, or close to it, allow you to feel like you're fulfilled far more often than you would if you didn't make any conscious effort to seek it, but the continual exercise will also have a lot of other benefits, too.

The first is that it will strengthen your faith, bring you closer to God, and give you strength when you need it most. This is perhaps the area of my life where I've felt the Lord's presence most keenly. Although I was raised in a churchgoing household, it wasn't until I reached young adulthood that I really began to understand the power of having God in your life.

In fact, the first time I felt truly shaken in my life was due to the loss of a close friend when I was a teenager. I hadn't dealt with death before, and certainly not in such a personal way. Suddenly I was confronted with doubts and emotions I didn't know how to make sense of. Everything seemed lost, upside down, and without meaning.

That was when I needed God the most, and luckily he was there for me to lean on. Through prayer, reflection, and the counsel of a pastor in my church, I was finally able to regain my bearings and move forward. The experience undoubtedly changed me in many ways, but it only made my faith stronger.

Over the course of the following years, that became a familiar pattern for me. From leaving home to join the Army to serving overseas and making a number of difficult career decisions, stress and fear were always met with calm and peace once I turned things over to God. Even now, my wife and I won't make a major financial or family decision without trying our best to understand what God's will is. And more times than I can count, we've been saved from major and minor disasters because of it.

Don't be fooled into thinking I had to learn this lesson just once, though. I still fall into the habit, sometimes, of waiting as long as possible before turning things over to God. The stubborn man in me wants to hold on to them, or try to control them, until I realize I simply can't. To personalize a famous Winston Churchill quote, *Tim Crain will always do the right thing – once he's tried everything else first.*

Because of the curiosity I have about other people's beliefs, and the relationships I've formed with other believers over the years, I sometimes attend religious services outside my own church. While I realize there are differences between Catholics and Presbyterians, for example, or Baptists and Episcopalians, I have found that we all have one thing in common: We know to turn to God when it matters most.

Regardless of the details that separate us, the understanding that faith is a centering force of strength always brings us together.

It would be a mistake to overlook the power and importance of that strength. At a time when so many in the world seem lost, walking aimlessly and searching for answers to questions they don't even understand, being able to turn back to your beliefs and know with certainty that you're headed in the right direction can literally be life-saving. It can give you the fortitude needed to turn your back on paths that aren't right for you, or to break away from harmful habits.

So even if you know this world is bound to cause you stress and distract you from God's path from time to time, know that bringing yourself closer to him is always worth the effort. It helps you create the foundation for a sense of spiritual peace that so many others lack.

For most of us, that would be enough. As it turns out, however, there are a lot of other tangible benefits to living in God's light, too.

Other Benefits of Being on the Path

I truly believe we all want to feel a sense of mental peace and purpose all at the same time. In that way, we are naturally drawn to God's light once we've experienced it, and are likely to try to seek it out again and again.

In the secular world, you'll often see people looking to fill the hole they sense in their lives. They'll do anything they can to get the sense of being "complete," even if they know on some level that their material pursuits are only going to bring them a momentary sense of satisfaction.

Believers don't have to waste their time chasing shadows. We can use our faith to find the fulfillment we crave.

But there are other tangible benefits that can help us in this world, too. Although many people (rightly) focus on the spiritual benefits of being close to God, it's only natural that being strong in your faith is going to spill over to other parts of your life, as well.

For instance, one of the most obvious examples is the way feeling rooted in your beliefs enhances all the other relationships in your life. When you feel secure in who you are, and in God's plan for your life, it makes it easier to be friendly, helpful, and more authentic than others. That means deeper relationships at work, stronger bonds with those you meet at church and in your personal life, and of course healthier marriages.

Psychologists will tell you that you can't truly love another person until you love yourself. I would take that one step farther and say it's easier to intertwine your life with another person's when you're both committed to Christ and willing to trust his plan for you. The resulting calm and confidence makes it easy for you to partner with and confide in one another and brings a sense of tightknit closeness that's hard to achieve any other way.

As I have loved you, so you must love one another.
— John 13:35

Because the bonds and friendships you form with others are such an important foundation in your life, and a building block of your happiness and fulfillment, strengthening them can only increase your feelings of peace and contentment.

Peace is easier to find when we feel hope for the future, which the Lord promises to us in Jeremiah 29:11. It is clear from this and other biblical references that hope is necessary to well-being. It's our light in the darkness. This light can help overcome some of life's challenges and struggles, especially when things seem bleak.

Faith and Material Success

Turning over your problems to the ultimate higher power, and trusting that you're going to get the answers or assistance you need, stops you from dwelling on that which isn't important or is beyond your control. And having a strong relationship with God can actually enhance your career and professional life, as well. There are a lot of reasons for this, and I find that they are occasionally misunderstood.

The first one is obvious but somewhat superficial: When you're part of a strong community of Christians, you're bound to form relationships with other successful people you can trust and turn to for counsel. Having mentors and supporters is important in any profession or industry, and an active religious and social life can help you expand your circle to include more people who can help you grow.

A second reason faith is good for your career has to do with the principle of certainty we already talked about.

Whenever I need to make a big decision, I pray that God will lead me into the direction I need and he wants. Rather than relying on just my own intuition, which can fail me, I have learned to trust him and accept that the right outcomes will happen.

That removes a lot of my doubt, of course, but it also takes away some of the stress and indecision that are so prevalent in nearly any kind of business or management position. More opportunities have been wasted by people waiting than they have from people making the wrong decision. In other words, making no move is often worse than making the wrong one, and having faith in God's plan for your life can spur you into action.

That brings us to what I consider to be the biggest reason, and the one that causes a lot of confusion: There are many principles in the Bible that lead us toward wealthy, prosperous lives if we're willing to follow them.

In my own family, we pray and meditate to ask for guidance frequently. When we do, we ask that God will show us his will and direct the outcome of events to achieve it. In other words, we don't ask him for what we want; we ask that he'll let us better understand what he wants for us or from us.

If you really want God to give you contentment, you have to be more interested in peace than you are things or achievements. He's willing to give it to you if you ask with an open heart.

I have often seen myself that God's peace is greater than what you can get from the perceived pleasures and luxuries of this world. Take, for instance, a boat my family bought years ago. To be sure, I enjoy spending time on it, cruising our way away from the shore and out into the open saltwater ahead. I often look forward to our boating time for days and weeks in advance.

The reality doesn't always live up to my excitement, though. For all the fun the boat can be, it can also bring its own share of headaches, particularly when it's broken down or the weather has changed and we find ourselves unexpectedly stranded.

In the end, those stormy evenings spent in hotels with my wife and kids, huddled around a board game or just talking about what's going on in our lives, are much more fulfilling to me than focusing on a material possession. When you're saving for a new car or a vacation home, it can be tempting to think that buying or achieving the "next thing" is going to bring you happiness. In reality, it's God's love and the peace he provides that have true value. Everything else is window dressing.

Knowing that, we have to balance our ambition for material success with our more important goals and purpose in this world. Doing so requires the right perspective.

In the same way that many people feel like the Bible promises a life of pain, anguish, and trial in this life for a reward in the next, they also tend to mistakenly believe that it encourages ongoing financial stress. I don't think that's the case at all. While we are cautioned against greed and dishonesty in many different books and verses, the Scriptures also say that wise people invest their talents and resources carefully.

Dishonest money dwindles away, but he who gathers money little by little makes it grow.
— *Proverbs 13:11*

Obviously, this verse isn't the last word on money and wealth from the Bible. God strongly cautions us against the love of money and acquiring wealth for its own sake. And yet, in the modern world there are uses for financial gifts. In the same way that some can give of their time or use their talents to further God's kingdom, others can use their money to help one another and do his work. In many cases, we can share some of our earnings *and* find other ways to contribute.

My conclusion is that we should never lust after money or let it be our master, but neither should we be afraid to put in hard work and save or invest in an honest, responsible way. I've seen time and time again that godly men and women have been able to take what they've learned in the Bible — lessons of hard work, faith, honesty, and perseverance — and use it to be successful in their careers.

The Qualities of Someone Who's on the Path

If I ask you to think of the most godly, trustworthy, and fulfilled people in your life, who comes to mind? Most of us have a handful of individuals who stand out for their honesty, their commitment, and the simple strength of their spirit.

Even though these men and women might be relatively rare, almost all of us know at least a few of them. Why is that?

One reason is almost certainly that people with a lot of strength and faith tend to be almost magnetic in their ability to draw others in and lead them. And they tend to make a strong impression on us because they seem to stand out with their energy, passion, and commitment.

These are people who are on the path already, and spending time with them is bound to make you want to imitate them, as well. Their happiness and fulfillment are contagious.

What do these people have in common? Here are just some of the qualities we tend to notice in them:

They are giving. Whether or not they have wealth and material success, they tend to always be giving to others. They share their time, their talents, their money, and their wisdom, using what God has given them to enrich other lives and show a way forward.

Psychologists and spiritual advisors agree: The more giving you are, both of yourself and what you have, the happier you tend to be. There's something special about sharing the gifts that come from us with others; the blessings seem to come back to us many times over.

They care for others and find ways to comfort them. In our world we're increasingly encouraged to think about ourselves, our own needs, and the minutia of our day-to-day lives. Yet those on the path practice what most of us experts would call empathy but is really just the habit of thinking beyond our own selves.

I learned long ago that few things are better for your mental health than helping someone else with a problem. Not only does it take your mind away from whatever might be bothering you, but getting a new perspective can also be the best way to appreciate what you already have – and the opportunity to reflect on how many people would love to trade places with you if they could only get the chance.

They are accommodating. In the same way, they avoid seeking the limelight or taking credit for successes that were truly group contributions. This makes them stand out because it flies directly in the face of the advice we seem to hear so often, which is to promote ourselves and stand up for our own interests out of fear that others won't do it on our behalf.

It seems like everyone wants to be famous, accomplished, and well known these days. The spirit of teamwork has been replaced by the cult of personality. But when others know you by your attitude and giving spirit, instead of your resume or highlighted accomplishments, they gain a new respect for the way you live.

They look for fairness and truth. Those in God's light are only interested in what's right, not necessarily what's easiest, quickest, or most convenient. Even though they have as many opportunities to take shortcuts as the rest of us, they avoid them at all costs because of the damage to their own spirit and credibility.

It seems like hardly anyone is who they seem to be anymore. Every week, we see another prominent person exposed as a liar, a hypocrite, or worse. And yet, in our own communities there are millions of people living their lives in accordance with their own values and principles, refusing to cut corners on their faith or principles.

They show mercy and compassion. The men and women we most admire aren't the ones who wield their power over others or can't wait to tell the people in their lives how right they were after the fact. Instead, they recognize that none of us is perfect, that everyone makes mistakes, and that the true measure of an individual is how they behave when there are no perceived consequences.

We all know how important it is to "be the bigger person" and how that can help us build our own self-respect over the long term. We also know how difficult that can be, especially in the heat of a difficult moment.

Exercising mercy and compassion are almost like skills in that they take practice and dedication. The rewards, though, are more than enough to justify the effort.

They are successful in overcoming temptation. All of us are tempted, of course, but what stands out is their ability to turn away from distractions instead of feeding them or holding on to them. They don't allow problems to grow and fester because they remain aware of their own weaknesses without dwelling on them.

This really comes down to discipline. It's difficult to overcome your biggest temptations if you allow them to come at you full strength every day. If you can make a habit of removing yourself from the wrong environments and situations, you'll find you are tempted less often. Holding on to something you know isn't healthy can be fun and even stress-relieving in the short term, but always leads to trouble later.

They work for peace and harmony. These people tend to be leaders, whether they are outgoing or in leadership positions or not, simply because they look for solutions to problems instead of escalating conflicts driven by ego or personal gain.

Although this may seem like weakness, the reality is it often takes more strength to let go and try to dissolve an argument than it does to hold your ground and push a disagreement forward or deepen a conflict.

They aren't afraid to stand up for what they believe. That's not always easy, especially in a day and age where Christians seem to be under attack from all sides. But they won't give in or allow their own faith to be questioned or belittled simply because *others* aren't choosing to walk in God's light.

They practice forgiveness. It's easy to judge others for what they've done or for the shortcomings we're sure they have. And yet, those who are on the path don't put themselves in the position of looking down on others. This also happens to be the perspective God encourages us to adopt, too.

There are a lot of biblical redemption stories. Paul himself was known as someone who killed Christians, until he later repented and became a leader within the church. In God's eyes, there is always time to change your course and come back. He can forgive sins men can't, and can welcome back those we could easily consider lost.

We are all called and invited into the kingdom. Even those who seem the farthest from the Lord's grace are missed at his table. Part of living on the path is remembering that our judgment of others isn't what matters. It is the Lord's table, after all, not ours.

In this way, men and women who are living in the light can serve as beacons and examples without coming across as preaching or self-righteous. They simply know where their faith and priorities lie and refuse to compromise on them to make others feel vindicated or comfortable.

If you're paying close attention, you might have noticed a couple of things about this list. The first is that the qualities tend to go hand-in-hand with one another. You rarely ever see a person with one or two of these gifts but not the rest. As I've already mentioned, holding on to your faith in Christ, and letting it fill you, tends to spill over from one area of your life to another. It's almost impossible to find peace without mercy, discipline, and perseverance, for example, just as you can't have the strength to stand up for your beliefs without also learning to love fairness and truth.

Another thing you might have gleaned, if you're an astute biblical scholar, is that these qualities can be associated with the Beatitudes as given by Jesus on the Sermon of the Mount. Given that the word "beatitude" itself derives from the Latin for "happiness," it shouldn't be surprising that Christians have long found them to be the qualities and ingredients of a fulfilling life. They are the outward signs that someone's on the path and living in a way that brings them peace, excitement, and contentment all at once.

I've already mentioned that many people tend to overlook the earthly gifts that come from heavenly principles sprinkled throughout the Scriptures. Because they focus on the laws, concepts, and details found within the Bible, they don't always see the advice for happy, healthy lives that's sitting right in front of them.

But, when we see the joy that those who are in the light have, it's only natural for us to be drawn to them and want to follow their example.

Living Away From God's Light

Although I've spent the majority of this chapter talking about the wonderful and positive ways that being on the path can enrich your life, your relationships, and even your health or your career, it's probably a good idea to point out that the opposite is just as true: When you *aren't* living your life in accordance with God's plan, you suffer the *absence* of those gifts.

In the next chapter, I'm going to explore the different ways that faith leads to inner peace. For the moment, however, it's sufficient to point out that the anchor of faith is a powerful one, and removing it can leave people feeling like they're drifting alone in a random sea of uncertainty. They don't have any context or frame of reference for the seemingly unexplained events they see happening around them and affecting their lives, and it can leave them feeling unhinged and out of control.

In the same way, they don't have relationships with God that feel solid, so the bonds they form with others suffer, as well. Their friendships are less stable, their marriages lacking trust and depth, and their partnerships tinged with the stain of uncertainty.

Because they can find themselves in a constant state of worry and despair, their health suffers in a number of subtle but profound ways, causing chronic illnesses and stealing their vitality away from them. They often feel like they lack purpose and direction, which impacts their ambition and professional lives. They suffer from indecision and inconsistent thinking, moving from one career project to the next hoping to finally discover something that makes them feel rooted in the world – even though they feel incapable of recognizing it right before their eyes.

And because they aren't enjoying those gifts of the spirit that believers are, they find themselves prone to jealousy, insecurity, self-promotion, argumentativeness, and a host of other problems.

Obviously, these are symptoms we can recognize in the world at large, but *we can also see them in ourselves*, especially when we let our faith falter and stop doing the work to bring ourselves closer to the Lord.

Just as living in God's light brings benefits that are hard to put into words, living outside of it can feel lonely and desperate in a way few of us would ever want to comprehend. Although it's a simple metaphor, it's an effective one: Living in the light is much better than hiding in the darkness.

As a Christian, you have already taken a first step in the right direction. The guidance you need is right in front of you, in the form of your Bible, your pastor, and others in your church, every day. For that reason, believers tend to be closer to the path than other people almost all the time, but your happiness and fulfillment aren't automatic. No matter how strong your belief is, there are always distractions and temptations waiting to pull you away in another direction.

> *Be alert and of sober mind. Your enemy the devil prowls around like a roaring lion looking for someone to devour.*
> *– 1 Peter 5:8*

You don't want to live away from God's love, but luckily you don't have to. It's up to you to decide whether you want to seek out his path for you and follow it or turn away. Knowing what's at stake, the decision should be an easy one.

IT'S ABOUT MORE THAN BELIEF

To be a Christian, you have to believe in the power of Christ. To truly seek the way, however, you have to go farther and actively embrace the gifts of peace, prosperity, and excitement that God is willing to put in front of you.

Making that leap is about more than belief in God; it's about putting your trust in what the Scriptures say. If you just pay lip service to what you hear on Sunday, then very little is going to actually change in your life through the week. If you're committed to altering the way you think, live, and treat yourself and others, you'll be amazed at what can happen.

Earlier in this chapter I mentioned that these aren't just ideas to me, but the blueprint for a happy, fulfilled life in Christ. I can't make you follow along, but I can tell you I've seen it work for myself, members of my family, and many of my friends, colleagues, and fellow believers.

It's true that God asks a lot from us in this life, but it's even truer that he gives us so much back in return. The only catch is that we have to trust him enough to follow along even when it feels like we're going against what we hear and see in the outside world. We have to put faith in the instructions he's given us rather than all the "noise" that surrounds us every day.

The world is a tough, chaotic place, but I truly believe that's because most people aren't centered and refuse to follow the path that's been set before them. The few that do – like the ones who stand out as the shining examples you thought about before – show us that it *is* possible to think, act, and live differently.

A better way of life is out there, one that brings you peace while making you feel engaged in the world. If you're ready to seek the way and find it, the next step is to look at how faith, peace, and purpose come together.

SEEKING THE WAY

✓ *How often do you prioritize material success over spiritual gifts?*

✓ *How would you explain the difference between belief and faith?*

✓ *Which people in your life show the qualities of living on the path, and why?*

✓ *How do you feel when you're far from God's path?*

CHAPTER THREE

Faith and Inner Peace

The fruit of that righteousness will be peace; its effect will be quietness and confidence forever.

— Isaiah 32:17

Although you may not realize it, you as a Christian have a head start over so many others when it comes to finding inner peace and satisfaction. That might seem obvious, but it's an important thing to keep in mind when it feels like life is overwhelming and you're nervous about the future.

I discovered a long time ago in my own life that faith in something greater than yourself is what keeps you rooted during times of stress, turmoil, and uncertainty. Yet for many people, the entire concept of "faith" is foreign, or even looked down upon. So they aren't just spiritually bankrupt in many ways, but are actively opposed to the one thing that could help them feel centered again.

In *Seeking Your Center*, I had to address this topic very carefully. On the one hand, I knew people needed faith to find the feeling of purpose and engagement I wanted to offer them. But on the other, I was keenly aware that talking too strongly or specifically about faith to an audience that wasn't ready for it could cause them to miss the bigger point.

In this chapter, I'm going to help you to understand the connection between your beliefs and the faith you have in them, and why it's so important to living life in God's light. And I'm going to offer you a few tips for strengthening your faith as you move forward.

Seeing Faith as a Journey

If Christians already have faith, why do I need to mention it at all?

For one thing, there *are* Christians who have, or practice, very little faith in their day-to-day lives. They have the kind of belief that's easy to talk about, but doesn't actually sustain them when things get tough. They may know they need to trust God, intellectually, but don't actually feel their faith or use it when the chips are down.

In fact, I would venture to say that a lot of us are like that in different times in our lives. Faith takes a lot of work; it needs to be strengthened. None of us is perfect when it comes to our track record of trusting in God's plans.

As humans, we almost never put enough faith in our Lord. In Mark 4:35-41, we are given the story of the disciples who are with Jesus in a boat when they come upon a storm. As the weather gets worse, they become agitated and afraid while Jesus sleeps.

Think about that for just a moment: Here are a group of men who have *the son of God next to them* and have seen him perform miracles. Despite that, their natural fear overrides their faith in the midst of a choppy storm. If the disciples couldn't keep faith with Jesus right there next to them, should we really be surprised that so many of us struggle to feel his hand in our daily comings and goings?

Of course, Jesus slept through the troubles because he already knew it wasn't an issue. The lack of faith his disciples had was the issue, not the actual thing they perceived to be a crisis. How often do we think we're in the midst of a storm when God could tell us we aren't really in any trouble? Why don't we trust his guidance and enjoy the peace he wants us to have?

I am frequently reminded that my own faith ebbs and flows. My desire is to continue to grow as a Christian, of course, and one of the ways I work at that is by praying continually. I don't practice *daily* prayer, which can often amount to "checking in with God" in the morning or at night, but prayer throughout the day whenever I feel like I need it. Doing so helps me find the faith and strength I need at the times it matters most.

In my military career, one of the interesting things I learned was that generals and commanders don't necessarily focus on innovation as much as they do execution. In other words, a big part of their job is learning to make fewer and fewer mistakes as they go through their career. I think that's a great analogy for the way believers have to approach their faith; we're all going to have moments of weakness, but they should become fewer and farther between as we walk the path that God has set out for us.

I want to challenge you right now to reflect on your own life and think about what faith really means to you. How often do you actually practice it, and can you truly say that your faith in the Lord is strong? Do you feel like it's leading you to inner peace?

Those are questions I can't answer for you, but they're incredibly important to you as you move through this journey. A belief in God is empty if it isn't backed by strong faith.

WE ALL NEED A HIGHER POWER

You don't even need to crack open your Bible or attend a church service to be reminded of just how much we need God in our lives – you just have to look through history.

Going back in time, you'll find that every civilization had a name for the divine. Although the details may have differed, all the world's great cultures (and all those that weren't so great) spent a lot of time looking for spiritual answers. The Egyptians and Greeks were known for their long religious ceremonies, and even ancient Native American groups with no written languages have records of their spirituality that still survive today.

Even now, non-believers often find themselves pulled into the exploration of spirituality, new age rituals, and metaphysical texts. Why is it that will toward God, or what someone *understands* as God, is so strong?

The reason is profound and simple at the same time: Simply acknowledging that there is a higher power at work in the universe lets you know that you're always loved and that most things in life are simply outside your control.

At first glance, that might seem like a daunting prospect. After all, wouldn't we all love to have more control over our lives and surroundings? Looking deeper, though, we can start to appreciate just how liberating it is. If God is steering the ship, then you don't have to try to control everything or get every decision right. Instead, you just have to listen to him and trust in his plan.

Additionally, having faith in something larger and more important than ourselves gives us a frame of reference for our ethics. The world doesn't always fold itself neatly into lines of ideas and activities that are "right" and "wrong." In fact, even spiritual leaders and biblical scholars can disagree about the meaning and intent behind various parts of Scripture. Still, having God's word to fall back on gives us a compass we can use to make the right decisions for ourselves and others when the answers we seek would otherwise be unclear.

Maintaining that kind of perspective can be helpful in the best of times and is an absolute necessity when we are experiencing lots of pain and stress. The more pressure is hoisted upon us, the more questionable our decisions usually become and the harder it is to find the right next step.

The one who gets wisdom loves life; the one who cherishes understanding will soon prosper.
— Proverbs 19:8

I've already mentioned how much easier it is to stay rooted in times of distress when you have faith in God, but the fact of the matter is that those moments aren't just limited to occasions where we are feeling pain. Even happiness and success can bring their own challenges and often require us to hold on to the right frame of mind when it would be easy to direct our thoughts elsewhere.

There's a reason so many people who are on the brink of losing everything with their health or well-being seek out God naturally, and why we actively encourage them to do so. Faith is an anchor that holds us in our spot when life wants to push us too far in any direction, whether that seems like a good change or a poor one at the moment.

Even those who haven't found Christ know they need to hold on to a higher power. For those of us who have been in his light already, it's even more important.

REAL FAITH IS PERSONAL

Lots of people have faith, whether they know it or not. Even many who wouldn't consider themselves to be spiritual believe in a guiding force that drives the universe. They may or may not consider it to be "God," but they *feel* the presence of something larger than themselves and are drawn to it.

That kind of faith is easy to have because it's instinctual. As Christians, we need to go farther and make our faith personal.

Within this context, I don't just mean having a personal relationship with Jesus Christ, as important as that is. What I'm getting at is a true, deep-down belief that God isn't just in control, but has a plan for your life – one that's specific to you, with your talents and situation.

> *For I know the plans I have for you, declares the Lord, plans to prosper you and not to harm you, plans to give you hope and a future. Then you will call on me and come to pray to me, and I will listen to you. You will seek me and find me when you seek me with all your heart.*
>
> *– Jeremiah 29:11-13*

Do you already believe that deep in your soul? If so, do you live in a way that's consistent with that belief?

If you aren't willing to follow God's plans, there's no telling what you might be missing out on. Take the case of Joseph, who was sold into slavery by his brothers because of their jealousy and ended up being second only to the Pharaoh in Egypt. To reach that point, he had to endure incredible pain and anguish, including a period of imprisonment.

Would you go through the same kinds of trials and tribulations if you felt they were part of God's plan for you, or would you look for a way to change your path?

For me, this is where the authenticity of your faith is truly counted and tested. It's the point where the rubber meets the road. If you say you have faith, which nearly every Christian would, but still worry about everything in your life, then you may not be putting enough trust in God.

I know I have been guilty of this at times in my own life. I can think of one occasion, when I was particularly down, that I found myself wondering whether I was really headed in the wrong direction – and if God was actually paying attention to my prayers.

In that moment, I happened to be spurred on by an inspiration to start making a list of all the things that were going well for me, or that I was thankful for. In under half an hour, I was able to count more than 130 different blessings that were working in my life. It suddenly occurred to me that even though I had wondered whether God was ignoring *me*, I had gotten the situation backward.

How often have you doubted God, when in reality you just haven't been paying enough attention to his guidance? What blessings have you received in your own life this year?

We simply cannot control all the things that are going on around us, even in our own lives, which is why it's so important to recognize that the Lord can steer you in the direction you need to be following. Otherwise, you're just following one random thought after another, hoping for the best.

That kind of real faith is more rare than you might think, however. In just a moment I'm going to give you a couple of examples to help inspire you and give some practical exercises I and others use to build up faith like a spiritual muscle that keeps you strong and at peace.

Before that, though, it's up to you to decide whether you actually have faith in God's personal plan for you and what you're willing to do about it if you don't. If you can't believe there's a plan for you, then everything else in this book is window dressing, regardless of what you believe.

The apostles said to the Lord, "Increase our faith!"
– Luke 17:5-6

It probably shouldn't be surprising that so many great leaders and influencers in history also had great faith. They didn't just believe in God, but also that doing his work, and trusting in his will, would lead to the right outcome even when the future seemed cloudy.

One of these great leaders was Abraham Lincoln, who despite not being thought of as one of the more religious U.S. presidents, nonetheless sprinkled his remarks and letters with numerous references to faith and Scripture.

After being tested through the death of his young son, President Lincoln sat over perhaps the most tumultuous point in American history, forced to watch the nation he was entrusted to lead tearing itself to pieces before his very eyes in one bloody battle after another.

Instead of getting lost in the stress and pressure of the situation, accounts from the time report that Lincoln would sink to his knees in prayer and find calm in it. In fact, in public remarks he made it clear that he was being led in the right direction rather than choosing it directly:

"Whatever shall appear to be God's will, I will do."
September 13, 1862[1]

"Amid the greatest difficulties of my administration, when I could not see any other resort, I would place my whole reliance in God, knowing that all would go well, and that He would decide for the right."
October 24, 1863[2]

---

1 Lincoln's Meditation on Divine Will
2 As reported from Lincoln's public remarks

Faith in History

These same thoughts echo through the surviving letters and remarks that remain from his presidency and point to an attitude all of us could stand to adopt. Even though we may never face the kind of crisis he did as president, it's easy to follow his example and trust God will help us manage our hardships, especially when they seem too heavy to bear on our own.

Because she was a Catholic nun, it's probably not surprising that Mother Teresa showed an extraordinary amount of faith in God and his mission for her life. Yet she still stands as one of the last century's most striking examples of what someone can accomplish with a little bit of faith and clarity in their purpose.

Acting on what she was sure was the Lord's instructions to her, she founded numerous shelters, programs, and protections in Calcutta for some of the poorest people on earth. As a result, she became known for her unrelenting passion and drive to help those less fortunate than herself.

In many ways, she stands at the complete opposite end of the spectrum from almost every traditional definition of success. She never earned a prestigious title and certainly didn't become wealthy. At the same time, however, she had the kind of spiritual success that few of us could ever hope to match. How many of us have ever accomplished even a small fraction of what she did?

Time and time again, she diminished her own accomplishments and instead credited her faith in God for helping her to make such a strong imprint on our world:

"I know God won't give me anything I can't handle. I just wish he didn't trust me so much."

"I'm a little pencil in the hand of a writing God, who is sending a love letter to the world."

"Prayer is not asking. Prayer is putting oneself in the hands of God, at His disposition, and listening to His voice in the depth of our hearts."[3]

As powerful as each of these statements is, though, they only serve as colorful little reminders of the way she lived her life. Her faith wasn't a show, an act, or even an attempt at believing – it represented complete devotion to God's will and a deep level of trust in his plan. She may have lived a very different life from Abraham Lincoln and faced a different set of challenges, but both used their deeply held beliefs to drive themselves forward when other paths would have been easier.

Going back a bit farther, we can find a fine example of utter, unshakable faith in Christopher Columbus.

---

3 Mother Theresa quotes courtesy of *Come Be Me Light: The Private Writings of the Saint of Calcutta*

Regardless of the role he actually played in the Americas, it's clear that he held very strong convictions about God's plan for him, to the point that he was willing to bet his life and future on them.

Columbus was born to a relatively poor and unremarkable family in Genoa, Italy, and many accounts point out his personal faith – and a desire to spread the word of Christ to new people – as one of the primary reasons for undergoing long voyages. Long before he arrived in the New World, he copied and carried his book of prophecies – Scriptures which he had copied by hand from his Bible into a notebook – meant to strengthen his beliefs and remind him of his purpose.

In addition, he was known for introducing religious practices to his crew, and in fact his first act upon sighting dry land was reportedly to lead a prayer.

Although historians have debated the long-term results of his ambitions, his faith in Christianity can't be questioned. He undertook long, gruesome, and incredibly risky voyages largely because he felt they were a calling issued by God. How many of us would be willing to do the same if it meant the possibility of illness, starvation, and never seeing our friends again?

I could of course include dozens of other examples, from the Bible and history, of people who not only had great faith in God but leaned upon it at crucial and pivotal moments. But this isn't a book about history – it's about changing your life, so I'll let these examples stand on their own.

What I want you to take away from them aren't historical facts and interesting conversation pieces, but the understanding that many, many great lives and accomplishments have been not just enhanced by religious faith, but actually based upon them. When you put your trust in the Lord, you make it possible to cut through so much of the spiritual clutter that often holds us back and make decisions that can have far-reaching consequences.

THE DIFFERENT LAYERS OF TRUST

Certainly, it takes a lot of work to build up the level of faith and trust that someone like Mother Teresa exhibited in her life. The first step is understanding that we may not trust God as much as we say we do or even as much as we *think* we do.

In fact, if we think about it, it's easy to prove that we don't. Although we might tell ourselves the right things or repeat what we hear in church, we often put more faith in worldly authorities than we do the ultimate authority.

For example, most of us trust doctors and lawyers. We put a great amount of faith in the government, and possibly even a specific political party. We show great faith in our employers, both as organizations and individuals who supervise us. We trust each other to drive safely on

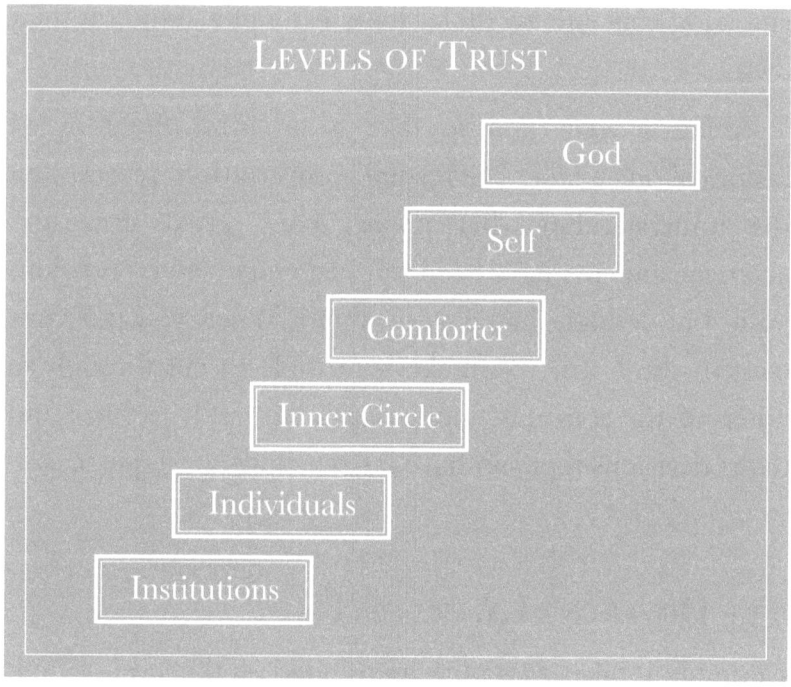

the highway, fulfill our professional obligations, or help us when we are in obvious need.

Each of these actions represents an inherent faith in *something*. And more often than not, we exercise this "everyday faith" a lot more than we do our trust in God. The most ironic and unfortunate part of that, of course, is that even the people and systems we trust most – those knowledgeable doctors, the established legal channels, and our economic foundations – occasionally let us down.

In fact, you could easily say that we as Christians tend to get things *backward* when it comes to trust. We put the most faith in things we can see and touch, even though they are the least deserving of that faith.

If you look at the graphic I've included, you'll get a sense of what I'm talking about. On the first level, we have companies, governments, and other institutions. The familiarity we have with them gives us a sense of trust, but it's important to remember that man-made institutions come and go, and may not always have our best interests at heart.

On the next level, we find individuals. In this case, we can think of them as "strangers on the street." We don't know them, and can't necessarily trust them, because we don't know anything about their character or values. Yet, the simple fact that they're humans with souls means we can probably trust them more than we can the nameless, faceless organizations we often deal with. While individuals may or may not have our own best interests at heart, most people will display a lot more empathy than we give them credit for.

Beyond that, we find our inner circle – the people whose love, advice, and opinions mean so much to us. Obviously, someone doesn't make their way into your inner circle if you don't trust them, so it goes without saying that you have a higher degree of faith in these people than you do individuals who would count as strangers or acquaintances. Still, we do need to be conscious of the possibility that we've misjudged someone in our inner circle or that they could make a mistake. Our faith in them should be firm, but not absolute.

Near the highest level of trust we find our comforter, who is our most trusted person. They represent our closest human relationship, and that bond grows stronger with the faith we have and develop in one another over time.

Near the top, we have the trust we place in ourselves. Regardless of whatever else we might think and believe, we trust ourselves more than we do any other person. As much weight as we put on our own opinions, though, we should always defer to the higher authority.

That brings us to our ultimate trust in God, in whom we should have faith above all. Our reliance in him should never waiver. His word and love are eternal, and his comfort is always there once we are ready to accept it. When you decide to step into God's light, great things can happen for you and others.

Strengthening Your Faith

Is faith something you either have or don't, or can it be developed and strengthened over time?

In my experience, it's definitely the latter. Faith really equates to trust, and that's something that has to be learned. The difference here is that instead of having someone else earn your trust, you have to learn to give up control and worry and turn things over to God.

That can actually be much harder than it seems or sounds. We live in a world where we are encouraged to be skeptical of everything, even feelings and emotions that seem to come from deep within us. That's especially true for our religious beliefs when they aren't shared by others.

The net effect of this is that our faith can begin to erode. In fact, this can happen without our even noticing. When it does, we say we have faith, and think we do, but don't genuinely feel it working in our lives. We talk about God, his love, and his plan, but don't actually trust in it in our daily lives.

Often, we make the outward statement that we trust in God's will for us. I want to challenge you to truly ask yourself, though, whether you put your faith in God when the chips are down and your confidence is waning. Are you really willing to turn decisions, and your worries, over to him? I suspect most of us are more attached to the illusion of control in our lives than we might be willing to admit.

If you suspect that might be the case in your life, don't despair. There are things we can do to actually build and encourage our own faith and let God into our hearts. I'm going to share with you some of my favorite techniques. Know that they work for me and probably will for you, too, but each of us is different. It's up to you to build faith in your own life the best way you can. Use my advice as a starting point, but don't be afraid to look for other habits and answers, as well.

Examining Your Faith

A good way to start is by asking yourself what you *really* believe. This might seem like an easy, natural exercise that would only take a few seconds, but I want you to go deeper than the surface. Rather than simply giving yourself the standard answers you normally would in everyday conversation, really stop and consider it. What is it, deep down, that you have faith in?

Most Christians wouldn't admit out loud that they place faith in certain parts of Scripture over others, or that they are more comfortable and rock solid with one area of their beliefs. But before you can take your faith to another level, you have to understand it in an intimate way. A few hours of reflection, and a bit of self-questioning and note-taking, can often reveal big insights.

Realizing that your faith isn't as strong as it could be doesn't necessarily have to reveal a weakness. It just means there are some areas of your spirituality you might need to work on or answers you still have to seek out. This can actually be exciting, rather than discouraging. Finding that your faith isn't as strong as it could be, and never will be, means there's always room for you to grow in your relationship with God and pull closer to him.

Make notes of the areas where your faith could be stronger, write down questions, and spend some time thinking about them on your own. Afterward, you might want to look through Scripture, meet with a spiritual advisor, or just have informal conversations with friends and mentors to get their thoughts. It might be difficult to express your own doubts or confusion at first, but you can rest assured that whatever your struggles with faith are, you won't be the first to have had them and you certainly aren't alone.

Also remember that our capabilities as human beings wax and wane. We aren't always going to be as strong as we'd like to be.

Fortunately, the Lord knows what's in our hearts and doesn't hold us to an unrealistic standard. Some days, I only have 80% of my faith, energy, and confidence to give. However, God sees me giving 100% of what I have available – even though the world would ask for the proverbial 110% at all times and all costs.

The idea that you're supposed to be perfect at all times leads to dysfunction and a sense of failure. God recognizes that weakness is an inherent part of the human condition. His measurement is different than the scale we use for ourselves, and that's unfortunate. In the world, we are programmed constantly to assume we have to be flawless to be loved, appreciated, and acknowledged. As believers, it's important for us to accept that God loves us exactly how we are, imperfect as that may be.

Building Faith Through Experience

I've already pointed out that faith is as much a habit as it is a feeling. I've seen his power work in my life in so many ways on so many different occasions. The same has probably happened for you more times than you can count. Why not use those experiences to reinforce your own faith on a regular basis?

Think back to times when you felt lost or confused, only to find God waiting to pick you back up once you put your trust in him. Consider making a few notes about the instances that stand out in your mind, making a special effort to outline the way you felt at the time and what the ultimate outcome was.

The righteousness is given through faith in Jesus Christ to all who believe.
— Romans 3:22

In ancient times, it was difficult to transmit information through writing because paper (or its equivalents, like parchment and stone) wasn't plentiful and many people couldn't read and understand what seemed like complicated words and symbols. So valuable information and perspectives were passed down from one group or generation to the next through stories.

Those stories kept knowledge and ideas alive. But they aren't just a tool for history. You have countless stories that make up your own past, as well. By expressing them, writing them down, and thinking about them critically, you can make it easier for yourself to look back and see what was *really* happening in the moment.

That can be the perfect way to explore your own faith without having to get through the fog and confusion that might surround your day-to-day life. Things might not seem clear now, but you can better understand what happened to you in the past, along with how you felt about it and what it did for your faith. Once you've shed some light on those experiences, you'll have a better sense of what's happening now and what is still to come.

You can keep refining this history, and adding to it, over time. Eventually, you're likely to discover a pattern: When you put your faith in God, you started to feel better and good things happened in your life (or, at the very least, you were able to understand and make peace with things you didn't expect). Now, consider the alternative. Where would you have been without that faith?

By writing these kinds of notes to yourself and looking them over when you feel like your faith isn't as strong as it could be, you can reinforce what you know and believe in your own soul. In other words, you can take what you've learned in the past and use it to remove doubts and fears when they are plaguing you.

Experience can be a great teacher, and faith can be learned and enhanced over time. So why not reinforce the lessons God has already brought you to move yourself closer to achieving inner peace in this life, regardless of what's happening all around you? God's action and support in your life are not just things to come. Your life has already been touched by his hand, whether you realize it yet or not.

Daily Affirmations

For centuries, Christians have been building their faith, and drawing a closer bond to God, through daily affirmations on love, peace, trust, and other spiritual principles.

There is any number of ways to build a library of affirmations. You could write your own, based on your favorite Bible verses. You could pull small bits of your favorite pieces of Scripture together and write them on notecards. You could even buy a set of pre-designed reminders, booklets, or even apps that give you biblical verses, history, and concepts you can look through every day.

It doesn't really matter which of these you choose, because they all essentially work the same way. And they *do* work.

The idea behind daily affirmations and readings – small positive reinforcements that build upon one another over time – is one of the simplest and most effective ways for people to learn, grow, and change. Consider that just 10 minutes a day spent on God's word each morning works out to one hour per week (assuming for the sake of simplicity that you skip your affirmations on Sunday and go to church instead).

That's not a lot of time. I advocate the "12 Cup" strategy that virtually anyone can fit into their schedule. It works like this: Twice a day, six days a week, a believer should sit down with their most important affirmations. For the sake of convenience and building a good habit, they can read through them with that first cup of coffee after they wake up in the morning and again with a hot cup of tea before bed in the evening.

No matter how busy you are, you could spare two five-minute blocks of time. As straightforward as it is, however, that simple act could have a huge change in any of our lives. Why? Because over the course of 12 months, that habit would equate to more than 50 hours of biblical knowledge and reinforcement.

In that amount of time, you could strengthen feelings of love and compassion, create a charitable mindset, break away from bad habits and temptations, and of course strengthen your faith.

Giving yourself 12 servings of Scripture per week is a small action, but it turns into a powerful habit. Any habit, and especially one that's so focused on God's word and our well-being, will eventually start to change thoughts and behaviors.

All too often, we think building a better relationship with God has to mean a huge, overwhelming effort. We think we need to go on long retreats or spend hours each day looking through verses. Those can be helpful things to do once in a while, but none of them is as effective as a simple, daily habit of reminding ourselves what God has to say about important subjects and instilling them in our thoughts.

To get even more from affirmations, practice writing them down, reading them out loud, or listening to them in audio format. Each of these engages the human mind in a different way and makes the message more memorable. So while reading is a good first step, experience your affirmations in different ways if you want to make them more powerful and significant.

Also, recognize that it sometimes takes a sharp ear to actually hear God's will. In my experience, a lot of believers expect to hear voices shouting down from the mountaintop when they need guidance. The Lord prefers to speak in light whispers. His comfort and instructions are there for you, but you have to be willing to calm your own wishes and expectations enough to understand them.

BE AROUND THE FAITHFUL

As a parent, it's easy to pick up on just how much your children can be affected by whom they spend time with. It's one of the reasons we worry so much when they seem to be "falling in with the wrong crowd."

Psychologists like to say our personalities are determined by the average of the five or so people we spend the most time with. That's probably overstating things just a little bit, but the fact remains that we are heavily influenced by our friends, peers, and family members – often more deeply than we realize.

This is an important realization when it comes to building faith, because one of the easiest ways to foster a stronger sense of belief is by surrounding yourself with other people who are strong in their faith, too. In other words, if the men and women who are influencing your personality tend to be rooted in their spiritual beliefs, they'll make you feel more grounded, too. On the other hand, if they are constantly questioning and filled with skepticism, it will be harder for you to remain rock solid in your own beliefs.

An easy way to surround yourself with the faithful is by spending more time at your church, in church-related activities, and/or with other believers in your life. These other believers can be business acquaintances, family members, or others. When that's not possible, you can make an effort to avoid people who are negative and tend to draw you into temptation.

While that might mean making some tough decisions in your life, it's often a matter of discipline — and frankly, better than the alternatives. Would you rather surround yourself with people who are positive and pick you up, making you feel like you're closer to your path, or spend your time with those who are miserable and want you to share in their pain?

Those who have true faith tend to be cheerful and giving. Those aren't just the kinds of people you want to emulate, but also the best ones to be around and spend time with.

Remember That Faith Is a Necessity

There's no doubt about it: Building faith takes work. It would be nice if it could just come to us telepathically, but for most people that's not going to be the case. You're going to have to cultivate it over time if you want to have it there when you need it most.

But, as with everything in this book, I can promise you that the end results are well worth the effort. Once you have faith deeply rooted in your heart, nothing can shake you from it. The world is always going to throw new struggles and challenges your way, but those who have faith also have peace and are equipped with the mental and spiritual tools to see the big picture (i.e., God's plan for all of us) and keep looking forward when it would be easier to get lost in grief or confusion.

I will listen to what the Lord says; he promises peace to his people, his faithful servants – but let them not turn to folly.
– Psalm 85:8

I like to think of faith as a kind of spiritual GPS. It can't always warn you about unexpected traffic or emergencies ahead, but it will keep you on course and give you a big-picture perspective when it feels like you aren't making any progress in your life.

There is absolutely no such thing as inner peace without some kind of faith, and the more faith you have, the easier it is to find. So if you want to stay on the path and walk in God's light, reinforcing your own beliefs isn't optional.

SEEKING THE WAY

- ✓ *How strongly do you believe finding inner peace is achievable in your life?*

- ✓ *How personal does your faith feel?*

- ✓ *Can you think of a few times when you didn't trust God as much as you do other people or secular institutions?*

- ✓ *What do you currently do on a daily basis to strengthen your faith?*

- ✓ *Do you surround yourself with other believers in your personal life?*

CHAPTER FOUR

Foundations of a Fulfilling Life

For God's gifts and his call are irrevocable.
— Romans 11:29

Although the Bible is a religious book first and foremost, Christians have known for centuries that it outlines the roadmap for a happy, healthy, and prosperous life as well. It's my belief that following these ideas also enhances us spiritually, since it's easier to feel connected to God when we are actively open to his plans for our lives and living in accordance with them.

In other words, when we take the Lord's advice, good things tend to happen for us. And when they do, we feel happier, healthier, and more spiritually fulfilled as a result. We are closer to the path, and that feeling inspires us to move even closer.

In this chapter, I'm going to outline our foundation and the four pillars of a fulfilling life, as given to us in the Scriptures and centuries of subsequent human experience. You'll notice that most of them come down to old-fashioned wisdom. That shouldn't be a surprise, since many of the most devout and spiritually rich people also seem to find success in other parts of their lives, too.

Note that these principles apply to every believer. In the next chapter, we are going to look at your personal values, gifts, and purpose, and then see how they all come together to bring you closer to peace, fulfillment, and joy in your life.

Your Foundation: Knowledge of God and His Word

In the beginning was the Word, and the Word was with God, and the Word was God.
— *John 1:1*

You can't love God and trust in his plan without knowing his word, and that means having a healthy amount of biblical knowledge and understanding behind you. Even if that weren't the case, reading and studying the Bible on a regular basis can have some wonderful side effects in your life.

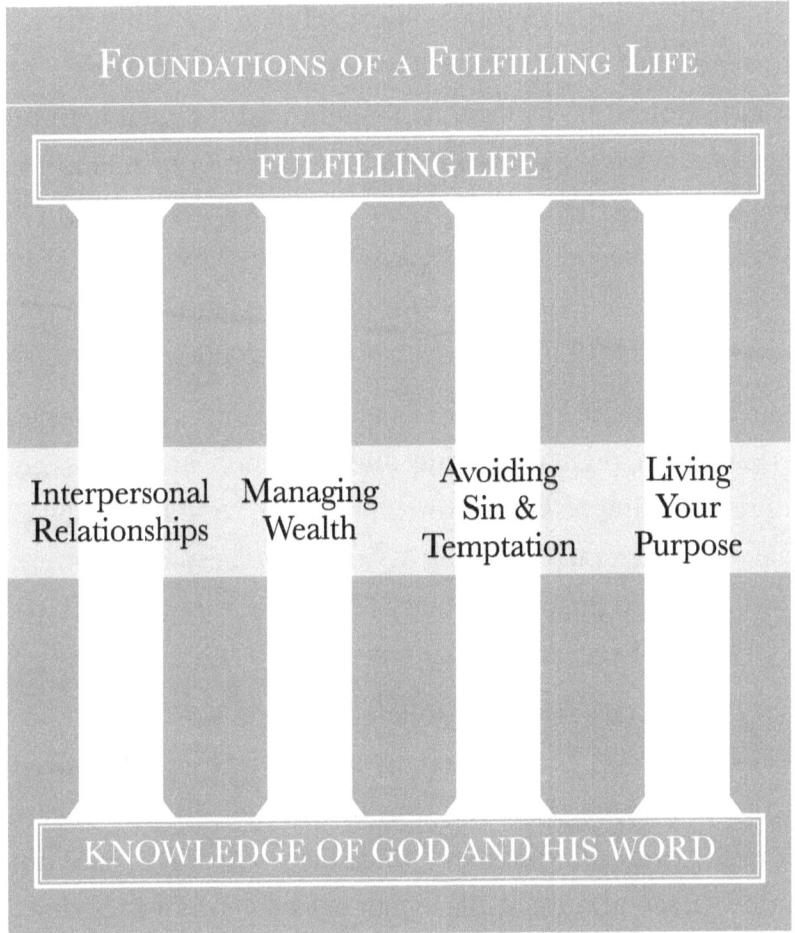

Before I get into the reasons why, let me take a moment to note that I'm not suggesting you need to memorize hundreds of verses or passages. As I've already admitted, I like digging into Scripture but I'm not the kind of person who can quote one section after another flawlessly from the top of my head. My mind just doesn't work that way.

Having the talent of biblical scholarship – the ability to read, memorize and retain the words of the Bible – is a gift. Not all of us have it, though, and the goal is to be led by God in your own life, not necessarily to memorize long passages. Being a biblical scholar is a great thing, but if you're like me, understand that it's okay to have a familiarity with Scripture that guides you down the path, even if you struggle to commit the exact words to memory.

The working knowledge I have of the Bible, for example, is based on regular reading and reflection and helps my understanding of God's word. I may not be able to tell you exactly where the Bible talks about forgiveness, for example, without peeking at my own copy for a few minutes, but I am conscious of its teachings and message.

Perhaps it's because so many of us are so busy, or because we've gotten used to having information given to us in bite-sized chunks on the Internet, but we have a larger group of Christians than ever who don't just not know much about the Bible, but actually admit they don't read theirs very often. But how can we grow as believers if we aren't familiar with God's word?

One way to increase your base of biblical knowledge is to simply choose a format that's easy for you to access and understand. For example, although I have many copies of the Bible around, I actually prefer to read and research sections through an app on my tablet. Scanning Scripture that way allows me to find what I'm looking for quickly, to search verses by topic or keyword, and even to get instant context for what I'm reading in the form of images, history, and related passages.

If bringing technology into the mix is important, so is choosing the right edition. I think some believers are put off from spending more time with their Bibles because they simply don't understand enough of the words they read. While the King James Version remains prevalent in many churches and is often quoted by those who are good at memorizing Scripture, there's nothing wrong with exploring different formats, especially if they speak to you more clearly.

I actually prefer a combination of a printed NIV copy and a searchable, interactive version I keep on my iPad. Not only does the combination of the two make it easier for me to understand without digging into phrasing from the middle centuries, but I can actually search for different topics, view accompanying maps and explanations, or even move through related passages that aren't next to one another.

Another possible reason believers put off studying their Bibles is they think it's not necessary. After all, if you go to church every Sunday and have your pastor or priest read Scripture to you, along with their own lesson or perspective, aren't you getting all you need already?

Certainly that's better than nothing, but it's not necessarily going to lead you to the verses, chapters, and lessons you need at that particular moment in your life. And, despite the best efforts of your spiritual leader, the limited time they have each Sunday means you could miss some important context that goes along with what you read. If nothing else, you're certain to get more from every sermon, lesson, and retreat if you're a regular Bible reader.

The spiritual battle we are in is a daily, minute-by-minute struggle. We need guidance and support more than once a week.

Imagine if you were to take an around-the-world trip on foot and had a handheld GPS to guide you, but could only check it once a week. It wouldn't take very long to go off course, would it? And how much more stress and difficulty would that add to your journey? When we neglect God's word, we're making things harder than they have to be and holding ourselves back from inner peace.

There is the perception that reading your Bible has to take a great deal of time – which it would if you sat down and took it in from start to finish in one sitting. But, as I hope you learned in my section on daily reinforcement, the key to building your faith and knowledge is consistency, not necessarily a massive initial effort. Make growing your biblical knowledge a priority, and it can become something you develop over time.

Enhancing your biblical knowledge doesn't just help you get more from church. The more you know, learn, and understand, the easier it will be for you to engage in religious discussions with friends and mentors (not to mention children and skeptical friends you might have), and the closer it will make you feel to God.

Plus, you'll often find that a bit of daily reading, even if it's seemingly random, will lead you to an answer or insight you've been looking for. Many, many times have I picked up my Bible, just opening to one page or another, and found a passage that related to a current struggle I was experiencing in my life. You can think of that as serendipity or divine will. Either way, it's great when it happens.

And finally, reading any part of the Bible can serve as a stand-alone affirmation, brightening your day and bringing you closer to the path all at once. Like a quick bit of exercise or an extra cup of coffee, the right verse can perk you up, decrease some of your stress, and either lift you up for the day to come or help you feel settled and relaxed at night.

INTERPERSONAL RELATIONSHIPS

For where two or three are gathered in my name, there I am among them.
— Matthew 18:20

I've already touched on the importance of surrounding yourself with the right kinds of people, and the topic of building healthy, affirming relationships is so important that I'm going to devote another entire chapter to it, as well.

For the moment, though, I just want to point out that you can't have a fulfilling life, or consistently feel like you're on God's path, without having strong connections to the most important people around you. Humans are social beings, and the Bible encourages lots of fellowship because having close-knit relationships adds an element to our lives that we can't get or satisfy in any other way.

We've already reflected on the fact that none of us can be at 100% all the time, whether it's physically, mentally, or spiritually. Luckily, God gives us others to lean and rely on, and to be there to pick us up when we have fallen and may not have the energy to get back up on our own.

That means having the right interpersonal connections needs to be a priority. But that's about more than simply surrounding yourself with the right people – you also have to build and sustain those bonds, giving them the same importance and attention you would your health or your career.

I think it's important to find these keystone relationships not just at church, but also in the workplace and elsewhere. For example, I know four people in my work who are faith-based. If I'm consciously aware of that fact, I can interact with them in a more intentional way and we can strengthen each other in our faith throughout the day. Whom do you know in your own life that you can use as a reminder of your beliefs, and vice versa?

What I'm really talking about here are two distinct but important steps. The first is to seek out relationships with other believers, or those who want to believe, whom you respect and admire. It's easy to spend a lot of time with those who are simply closest to us, in a physical or metaphorical sense, even if they aren't necessarily the best influences on our lives.

The second, more difficult step is to actively reach out and make plans to get together with them. It can be easy to come home from work and simply crash on the couch, for example, when your time would be better spent playing basketball in the driveway with your kids. Or you can schedule a weekend fishing getaway with old buddies rather than letting those relationships grow more and more distant.

The funny thing about these sorts of situations is that they often feel like chores or inconveniences at the time, when our minds and bodies are tired and tell us they'd rather switch off, but they can end up being among the most energizing and fulfilling hours we spend each week. They are the moments that make us feel happy and connected, rather than isolated and alone.

Another point to make about interpersonal relationships is that different people fill different roles in our lives. No one should be expected to cover them all, and we need to have individuals who mean different things for us if we are to be happy, connected, and grounded.

For example, your spouse or romantic partner is almost always going to be one of the most important people to you, and an incredibly strong influence. But that person can't meet all of your interpersonal needs, no matter how wonderful they are. Having a close friend, a mentor, and a spiritual advisor are all necessary, as well. Just as these people play different parts in your life than your wife or husband might, you fill different needs for them, as well.

Put together, all of these interpersonal relationships are as important to us as the food we eat or the air we breathe. In fact, a healthy social life is tied to longevity and improved physical well-being, making it an important aspect of your life.

Not all of your connections and relationships have to be formal, however. Time and time again, I've come into contact with groups of believers who get together to pray or share ideas. They might not be in a traditional church setting or even have a specific goal, but they're engaging in the kind of fellowship that's nurturing to everyone involved.

People are designed to need one another, and the strong connections we have between us bring us closer to God's light. Are you putting enough work into building and maintaining the interpersonal relationships that bring happiness to your life?

Managing Wealth

As goods increase, so do those who consume them. And what benefit are they to their owners except to feast their eyes upon them?
— Ecclesiastes 5:11

I think a lot of people tend to misunderstand the concept of wealth, both in general and from a biblical perspective. You shouldn't need a set of Bible verses to tell you that a love of money isn't just unhealthy, but is actually incredibly unfulfilling.

In the secular world, there is a common misconception that just having a little bit more in your bank account can make you happy, healthy, and wise. Unfortunately, that's never the case — instead, chasing after money only leads you toward a hollow search for *more* money, which becomes fruitless and empty very quickly.

Even Christians aren't immune to this delusion, and greed for its own sake can be more common than we'd like to admit, even among churchgoers. We are cautioned again and again in the Bible to avoid wealth for its own sake and cautioned against confusing wealth with wisdom.

As humans, we are good at seeing problems and trying to imagine solutions for them. In many ways, these analytical gifts are a good thing – they've led to things like indoor heating and plumbing, as well as agriculture and social services.

However, those same analytical, problem-solving traits can lead us into trouble, too. The fact that money can be counted makes it an appealing topic (and potential solution) to our human minds. For instance, we tell ourselves, "If I could get rid of this bad car with more money, my problem would be solved." That's only true in a very immediate sense. At a certain point, solving a perceived problem only leads to the identification of more problems – the "need" for a new car leads to the "need" for more wealth or a vacation home.

In other words, there's always something new to count, assess, or spend money on. The problems to be solved never go away because they are a feature of the human mind.

Whoever loves money never has enough; whoever loves wealth is never satisfied with their income.
– Ecclesiastes 5:10

In this case, simply following Scripture could help you avoid making the same mistake as countless others have and give you decades' worth of wisdom in the process. No one ever got happier chasing money, but lots of lives have been ruined in its pursuit.

However, I don't necessarily feel like God wants us to struggle financially, either. For one thing, continual pain and turmoil go against the sense of peace and contentment we are seeking. And for another, money can be useful for things other than meeting basic needs, like committing acts of charity or investing in our families and faith.

So how do we find the answer to this conundrum? How do we enjoy the gifts and wisdom that are in front of us without falling into the trap of sacrificing ourselves and our spiritual well-being for the sake of a few extra digits in our bank accounts?

Keep your lives free from the love of money and be content with whatever you have.
— *Hebrews 13:5*

I think the key is to think not in terms of amounts, but intent. The Bible warns us about hoarding money, feeding our greed, and falling into sin for financial gain. It also extols the values of hard work, prudence, and careful saving.

Knowing that, I think any Christian can feel good about working hard, making an honest living, and planning for the future. By doing so, we are free to prosper without engaging in behaviors that go against our faith or cause us to lose respect for ourselves. We can accumulate modest amounts of wealth so long as we don't let it become the focus of our lives.

Earning money, of course, is only half the issue. There is also the concern about how we spend and share it. The Bible has a great deal to say on this topic, as well.

Remember this: whoever sows sparingly will also reap sparingly, and whoever sows generously will also reap generously.
— 2 Corinthians 9:6

And everything I did, I showed you that by this kind of hard work we must help the weak, remembering the words the Lord Jesus himself said: "It is more blessed to give than to receive."
— Acts 20:35

Again, these are only two representative verses from a large body of Scripture, but the message is clear: As believers, it is incumbent upon us to share what we have with others, and especially those in need. Some will have the special talent and gift of making money. They can use it to further the kingdom, just as others use their talents for teaching, artistry, or sharing the word to enhance God's glory.

Giving money, to our churches and other causes, is one of the ways we show and spread love throughout the world. We give of ourselves, instead of holding on to that which we earned or gathered, because it helps others and enriches our own lives at the same time.

I also believe each of us is called upon to support unique causes or individuals in need on an individual basis by God. Think of a time in your own life when you were traveling and saw someone who could use help, but it seemed like you were the only one who noticed or cared about that individual or situation. Maybe that's God trying to tell you that a particular problem is yours to solve, and you should take action.

I can remember one occasion when my wife and I were in a large grocery store. We happened to pass a young man with a few items in the bottom of his cart as we made our way from one aisle to another. Just as we were walking away and beginning to look for the next set of items on our list, Amy stopped, grabbed me by the arm, and whispered, "Something is wrong."

I asked if she was sure, and she was. Something drew her back to the previous aisle, where we now noticed the young man was weeping. He was in great distress because he didn't have the money he needed to feed his family. Although he had just finished his education at a technical school and gotten a job, he hadn't received his first paycheck yet.

Another shopper had noticed his pain, as well, but had responded by berating him for purchasing what she had decided were unhealthy foods for his young children (which, incidentally, were among the few items he could afford).

Amy's heart was very touched by his dilemma, and after the other shopper had finished her lecture, we made a quick decision to help him get the groceries he needed. Afterward, we drove the young man home (he'd come on the bus) and wished him well. When we were about to leave, he ran from his house and stopped us. With tears in his eyes, he hugged my wife and shook my hand, letting us know how important our support had been.

As much as we appreciated his gratitude, I wanted him to know that it was God who was responsible for helping him, and not us.

Those weren't just words. I truly believe the Lord put us in a place to be able to be of assistance to someone in need at that moment, and we were just fortunate enough to hear his instructions. If you're listening, you'll undoubtedly come across countless opportunities to do the same in your life.

The human need to give and share is strong. We see this in the intentional giving of gifts around the world and even in secular homes and organizations. From Red Cross donations for disaster relief to charitable drives around the holidays, the inclination to give to those who need help is an inherent part of humanity. We just know, deep down, that it's the right thing to do and an important step on the path to happiness.

You don't have to empty your checking account every time someone asks you for money just to walk on God's path, of course. We are all given different talents, and the ability to earn money is only one of them. In the same way that some of us are blessed to be scholars who can memorize Scripture, and some (like Mother Teresa) can offer time and compassion, others will be given an opportunity to contribute to the kingdom financially. The key is to understand what God's plan is for your life and how your talents are best used.

Going through your life with a charitable spirit, and remembering that many, many people don't have the gifts and blessings that you do, is important. We should never love money so much that we are willing to do anything to get it, or that we are afraid to part with some of what we have.

As I said, this piece of good and lasting advice isn't just based on biblical passages or spiritual edicts – it's also one of the most important principles to enjoying a happy, balanced life in which you're satisfied with what you receive.

Although the very concept of "sin" has huge overtones, I often find that the kinds of things believers struggle with don't involve murder or adultery, as examples, but everyday sins that reflect a lack of discipline as much as they do a desire to defy God.

In other words, a lot of sin is like binging on candy or fast food – instantly gratifying but ultimately painful or harmful. We do things even though we know better because we think they'll relieve pressure or give us some small relief in the short term.

Ironically enough, that also tends to make them harder to overcome. Most of us already know not to commit what we perceive as "major" sins, but we don't necessarily have the strength to stop committing the ones we think are "minor."

The first step to overcoming your sins is recognizing what they are in an honest, straightforward way. This is yet again another area of your life where journaling and recording your thoughts can be important and beneficial.

Before you can admit your sins to another person, you have to face them on your own and be honest with yourself about the times when you've come up short. You also have to recognize the temptations that are likely to cause you problems again in the future, and the circumstances that led you to give in. Sometimes, it's not even clear to us how or why we did something wrong until we look at the situation later on. Then, we can see where we erred – and more important, how we can avoid doing so in the future.

The same kinds of slight modifications can often be helpful for overcoming jealousy, envy, lust, and other common sins that plague us. Trying to defeat them all at once can feel overwhelming, but making little changes that put the temptation "out of sight and out of mind" makes the process easier.

Another thing you can do is talk through your sins and temptations with another person. This doesn't necessarily have to be in a formal, confession-like setting if that's not in your faith. Just talking about the problem with another person can help you to overcome it.

Avoiding Sin and Temptation

It kind of goes without saying that it's going to be hard for you to walk on the path of God's plan for you if you're constantly indulging in grave sins or succumbing to temptation. None of us is perfect, of course, but neither can we experience peace and feel strong in our faith if we can't manage to obey the commandments and stop ourselves from doing things we shouldn't.

Many times, admitting that we're having trouble to another person eases the burden. They can understand our pain, provide a bit of feedback, and maybe even share a story or two from their own lives that helps move us in the right direction.

Discussing temptations with others also works because we all tend to change our behavior when we become accountable for an action or specific result. In other words, if someone close to us (like a spouse, mentor, or spiritual advisor) knows we're struggling with something, they can help us to avoid tricky situations and keep tabs on our progress. Just knowing that we will have to admit to something later is often reason enough not to do it in the first place!

Whoever conceals their sins does not prosper, but the one who confesses and renounces them finds mercy.
  — *Proverbs 28:13*

As important as it is to share your sins and be accountable, however, I personally believe this is best done with those who are close enough in your life to trust. Public confessions are interesting, but they can quickly turn into something that seems more like a hearing, an interrogation, or even a contest. No one wins when believers are shamed, or when they seem to be trying to one-up each other to prove who has been the biggest sinner in the past.

You can also remove temptations by crowding them out. That is, follow the tactic of using daily devotionals and other forms of positive encouragement on a regular basis and you may find the urge to sin is simply less strong than it was before. That's because your mind is filled with so many positive thoughts that it has less energy left to hold on to negative ones. Again, this is the very essence of simplicity at work.

And finally, you can stop yourself from making a bad decision simply by thinking through the consequences. How will you feel later — mentally, spiritually, or physically —

if you follow through on a temptation? Will you feel proud and energized, or weakened and discouraged? There are consequences to every action, and remaining aware of them is a good way to break bad habits.

When it comes to sin, a lot of people (and even Christians) tend to think of biblical commands and instructions as a giant "do not do" list. They consider them a set of forbidden ideas and activities that are almost arbitrary.

When you look closer, though, you find that avoiding sin isn't about making God happy, but following the warnings he has given so each of us can live a happier, more content life. The commandments aren't arbitrary; they are there for our own benefit. There isn't a single sin you can commit that's going to make you feel better, or more at peace, in the long run. If you can remember that, and know that the Lord only wants what's best for you, the temptations you face on a daily basis will seem a lot less appealing.

Finding and Living Your Purpose

Each one of us is born for a reason. We all have a purpose, along with unique skills and talents that allow us to fill the role in God's plan for our lives.

While that might sound constraining, it's actually liberating. When you discover something you're good at – a task or role that allows you to excel while contributing to the greater good – it feels fantastic.

We all know people who seem to have simply "found their niche" at some point in life. They can usually be found at the top of their fields, they are less stressed and more creative, and they take genuine joy in their work. The same thing can happen in our private lives, too. When we discover something that not only we are interested in but is also a great match for our innate talents, it turns into the perfect fit of fun, relaxation, and fulfillment.

Remember that "discovering" doesn't necessarily mean "discovering right away." Sometimes in life we experience challenges, or difficult pathways, that don't seem to make any sense at the time. In the end, we often find that God has been leading us in a different direction so we can discover our true purpose, even though it wasn't obvious at the moment. I know that in my own life, I've found myself in challenging work or personal situations that seemed to be going nowhere. Only later was I able to realize that God was leading me to a place where my talents could be better leveraged or toward a situation where I would ultimately be much happier.

Interestingly, though, it's always clear in retrospect that God's plan was better than my own. Left to my own devices, I would probably do the easier thing more often than not and try to avoid uncomfortable decisions or life changes. The Lord has much better vision than we do, of course, and knows that our true joy may lie just on the other side of a current difficulty. By avoiding the rough patches and ignoring his guidance, we risk missing out on the satisfaction he has planned for us.

In many ways, discovering your purpose, and learning to live within the role the Lord has planned for you, is the key to combining excitement with contentment. Although those two emotions aren't normally thought of together, they certainly can be when you're engaged in an activity or position that almost literally pulls you out of bed *and* makes you feel good about the result at the same time.

You'll notice that both of those elements usually need to be in place for you to move on the path. Some things are fun and exciting, but are ultimately unimportant in the grand scheme of things. Other activities we do because they are important, even though they don't bring us much in the way of joy or entertainment. There will always be a place in life for both, but it's the intersection that leads to true happiness, especially at work, in a vocation, or in a volunteer situation.

As an example, a skilled surgeon might enjoy the mental and physical challenges of the job, but also love the fact that they can help save lives. A volunteer who builds homes can derive pleasure from the simple act of constructing walls, doors, and windows, but get an even greater satisfaction from knowing they've helped shelter a family in need. A teacher can enjoy working with students while being proud to help shape a new generation of young minds. A young mother might live to see her child smile, but also feel enriched by the close bonds she fosters within her family.

The examples can go on and on. The point isn't for you to see yourself in any of these, however, but to realize that each of us has several unique and distinct things we can do that most others can't do the same way, or at the same level. Finding how that aligns with the rest of the world, and God's plan for us, is like uncovering a hidden joy.

So I saw that there is nothing better for a person than to enjoy their work, because that is their lot. For who can bring them to see what will happen after them?
— *Ecclesiastes 3:22*

In the next chapter, we are going to explore the ways you can discover your purpose. You may find that you have more than one, and even several, or that they change over the course of your life. What matters isn't that you have a firm job, vocation, or skill in mind, but that you always look to maximize your talent and be open to the roles you want to fill.

Many of us tend to think that "doing nothing" or having the freedom to "do whatever we want" would be the ultimate luxury in life, but those who achieve the means to live in leisure are rarely satisfied. That's because the key isn't to avoid hard work, but to find the kind of work that feels joyful and meaningful to you.

That's why you see so many very successful men and women who continue working right up until the day they die, or at least staying active in some kind of career – being engaged and having a purpose is much more satisfying than wasting your days in a constant state of vacation. Occasional breaks can be good for your mind; being permanently idle is bad for the soul. The reason is because we're here to serve a purpose and make a difference. That work continues throughout our lives without an end.

For the sake of clarity, understand that I'm not suggesting you have to work in your current job, or stay in your career path, until the day you die. What I am hoping is that you'll see your life and purpose as a journey and that you'll keep looking for opportunities to fulfill your purpose within God's kingdom throughout your life.

Without a purpose, we are confined to merely surviving by going through the motions. That's not what God has designed us for, and it's certainly not what's going to bring us into his light.

Filling in the Gaps

Usually, when we feel like we are far from the path, it can be traced back to a gap in the foundation of belief or the four pillars. Without any of them, our lives feel a little bit empty and unfulfilling.

That shouldn't be a surprise. Having knowledge of the word is important to growing your faith, and you'll never know God as closely as you'd like to without it. Interpersonal relationships strongly influence our mood and health, and we need people to fill the most important roles in our lives and have an innate desire to fill those for others in return. Working only for money or hoarding our wealth is a sure path to unhappiness. Succumbing to temptations erodes our faith and self-confidence, and finding your purpose is an essential ingredient to happiness.

Even with the foundation and pillars in place, though, we still have a couple pieces of the puzzle to fill in. That's because everyone is a little bit different, and what you need for your life might not be exactly the same as what I need for mine. That's the dilemma we'll explore in the next chapter.

SEEKING THE WAY

✓ *How often do you read God's word? What could you do to develop a working knowledge of the Bible?*

✓ *How big of a priority are you making the important relationships in your life?*

✓ *What is your attitude toward wealth? How was wealth or income discussed in your home growing up? What was behind family behaviors and norms?*

✓ *Which sins are particularly troublesome for you? How do they make you feel like you have no power to control them?*

✓ *How strongly do you feel that God has a purpose for your life? How close are you to living your life in a way to serve that purpose?*

CHAPTER FIVE

Your Values and Purpose

We have different gifts, according to the grace given to each of us. If your gift is prophesying, then prophesy in accordance with your faith; if it is serving, then serve; if it is teaching, then teach; if it is to encourage, then give encouragement; if it is giving, then give generously; if it is to lead, do it diligently; if it is to show mercy, do it cheerfully.

— *Romans 12:6-8*

There are more than 7 billion people on planet Earth, and we're all different. Some of us might look or sound alike, but our genetics, experiences, and personalities are as unique as snowflakes.

Sometimes, it seems like life would be a lot easier if we would all feel, think, and act the same way, yet that's just not how we are wired. Have you ever wondered why that is? I think it's pretty clear we're different because we need to be. God has different jobs and roles for each of us, and that means we can't all conform to the same mold.

The differences go beyond our skills and talents, though, and extend into values and preferences. That means activities and situations that are going to make me feel joyful and content might not be as fulfilling for you, and vice versa. So if we want to accept the happiness God is offering us in our lives, and make full use of our gifts, then we have to know a little bit about ourselves first.

In this chapter, we're going to explore your values and purpose. Although those might sound like very big terms, the idea is simple: We want to get to the core of what makes you unique from everyone else, and then use those insights to build a life that's fulfilling. We want to learn what makes you happy, but also where you fit in God's plan and how you can live out your purpose in an engaging, satisfying way.

Your Personal Values

In the last chapter we looked at the elements of a fulfilling life that can help bring you closer to the path. They are proven principles that aren't just referred to again and again in Scripture, but also have been shown to be important to happiness for people in any culture or setting throughout history.

Your personal values are related to these, but aren't necessarily the same thing. An easy way to think about this would be your tastes in food. We all need sustenance to survive, but some of us prefer hamburgers to spaghetti. One is a broad requirement, while the other is specific to an individual.

In the same way, we all have certain things we need to be happy, content, and engaged in our work, our personal lives, and our faith. But there are also special hopes, wishes, and passions that are specific to each of us. I'm going to call those values in this book because they are stronger and more important than simple preferences, but don't get hung up on that word. While some of them truly are values (like a love for spending time with your family), others fit a little more loosely under that umbrella.

For example, I count "adventure" as one of my values. If I don't do something that gets my pulse up once in a while, it tends to affect my mood and productivity. So while "thrill-seeking" might not be something people think of as a traditional value, it's incredibly important to my life, albeit in small, occasional doses.

Even though flying small airplanes might not be specifically referenced anywhere in the Bible, I find it's nonetheless one of the jobs God has built me for. It helps me function at a high level and could let me do some of his work later, perhaps as a volunteer or part of a mission to an area needing disaster relief.

Other personal values could include learning, exercising, or even enjoying laughter. Keep that in mind as we move through some of the following topics and exercises – not all of your values have to be rigid or serious. We're looking for the qualities that make you a unique person, not necessarily to identify something that falls into a definite category.

IDENTIFYING YOUR VALUES

There are different kinds of gifts, but the same Spirit distributes them. There are different kinds of service, but the same Lord. There are different kinds of working, but in all of them and in everyone it is the same God at work.
— 1 Corinthians 12:4-6

Before you can incorporate your values into your life, and pull yourself closer to the path, you have to know exactly what they are.

In theory, finding your own values should be as simple as writing out a list and then prioritizing your answers. However, most people find that the exercise actually takes a bit more work than that. As it turns out, most of us have a more complicated value structure than we first realize.

This is partly because of the reason I've already given: A lot of the preferences and priorities that go into making a happy, fulfilled life don't necessarily fall into the category of "values," or at least they don't in the traditional sense. But they're still important and need to be counted and understood.

Another reason is that some of our values and motivations may be subconscious and actually hidden from us. For that reason, it can take a little bit of work to draw them out and understand them.

There are formal and informal ways to address this problem. I'll begin with the easiest, which is simply to start journaling and reflecting back on your life. Think about the things that really make you feel happy and satisfied, as well as the times when you felt excited, fulfilled, and fully engaged in what you were doing. Chances are, the types of challenges and experiences that come to mind fall squarely into your core values.

Another technique is to ask friends, family members, and mentors to see what *they* think your values are. Sometimes, our most important qualities are easy for others to spot but difficult to recognize in ourselves. Asking for their honest input can be a great way to fill in gaps in our understanding.

And finally, you can turn to professionals. This is a topic I'll be coming back to in just a moment, so I won't say a lot on it now, except that it can be difficult to know your own mind and sometimes an outside perspective can be helpful, particularly if you feel a lot of confusion about your own values and priorities.

Common Personal Values

Although we all have our own sets of values, many of us have goals, dreams, and passions that fall into a few broad categories, such as:

Family and Relationships	Encouraging and Comforting
Professional Success	Leadership
Missionary Work	Trust
Leisure Time	Forgiveness
Fitness and Health	Singing and Music
Competition	Loyalty
Learning	Humility
Charity and Giving	Wisdom
Mentoring	Autonomy
Christian Scholarship	Honor
Caring for Others	Structure
Professional Leadership	Acceptance and Equality
Teaching and Guidance	Hospitality
Offering Comfort and Compassion	Study
	Religion and Church
Research and Discovery	Spirituality
Creativity	Love
Building	Adventure

By using these as a starting point, you may be able to uncover some of your own personal values and understand them better. Again, I should point out that yours might not only be different, but also more specific. For instance, it might be important to you to understand the differences between different versions of the Bible or translations of Scripture between different languages. That falls under the broad category of scholarship, of course, but it's about finding the answers that are right for you.

The same goes for a value like family and relationships. Perhaps one of your priorities is to spend a quiet night at home with your spouse each week. Another related priority could be to visit your parents in another state once every three months. Even though these two goals fall into the same broad category, they are really separate things. Likewise, you may have a lot of values around charity and giving, but few or none around fitness. Don't feel like you have to include everything; just look for the answers that are right for you.

Realize that every one of these passions and talents has been put into your heart by the Lord. None of them is an accident. Even if they don't necessarily seem relevant to your life right now, they may have been put there so you can ultimately do something important to support the work of God's kingdom. The more you understand and explore them, the closer you can come to fulfilling the true purpose that has been given for your life.

Although journaling is important for virtually any step in this journey, identifying your values is one place where a bit of written self-reflection can be especially crucial. No matter how well you think you know your own values, you might be surprised at what pops into your mind, especially if you haven't done this kind of exercise before or haven't done it in a while.

Pulling Your Life Into Alignment

Identifying your values can be hard work, but it's only one part of the process. The next step is to determine which parts of your life are in alignment with your values and which ones aren't.

An easy example is the all-too-common trade-off between professional success and family life. Being good at what you do is probably important to you. But is it more important than spending time with your kids? If one of your values is getting all your attention while others are being completely ignored, you're always going to feel disgruntled, off-balance, and out of touch with your true nature.

That doesn't necessarily mean you have to make drastic and instant changes in your life, but that it's important to realize the Lord put you on this earth with specific skills and tastes for a reason. If you're neglecting some of your passions, and especially your biggest core values, you're probably not doing any favors for yourself, your faith, your loved ones, or the ones you were meant to impact.

When we ignore our values, we open the door to fatigue and frustration, which can make temptations seem stronger than they actually are. The more fulfilled and content you are with your life, the less likely you are to fall into sin and doubt. Why make yourself unhappy when it isn't good for you in the long run?

We'll talk about what you can do to change your life and move closer to your path in a coming chapter. For the moment, though, it's important that you understand your values, recognize them for what they are instead of what you might want them to be, and know that even though lots of them are fairly universal, your specific set of values and priorities is unique.

With that understanding in place, we can turn to the other part of your personality that's so important to moving you into God's light – your purpose on earth.

Understanding Your Purpose

If your values are what you love, your purpose is what you're built to do.

The two are definitely closely related, but aren't exactly the same thing. Values largely come down to passions and priorities, while your purpose is the sum of your natural talents, abilities, and ambitions *combined* with those values.

Or, to think of it a little more simply, it's the intersection of what you love to do and what you're great at doing.

It has been said that being able to do whatever you want is freedom, and loving what you're doing is happiness. I'm not sure there's a better way to introduce this subject, since fulfilling our purpose – both in our lives and in God's plan – brings us excitement and fulfillment in a way that few other things can.

This is a big topic, and one that's integral to your happiness, so let's look at a few important details and caveats...

Your Purpose Is Bigger Than Your Career

It's important to note that discovering your purpose isn't necessarily the same as finding the right job or career path. The two are very often interrelated, in that having employment that aligns with your purpose is a great blessing, but we shouldn't confuse one with the other.

Some people have a vocation or calling that doesn't have anything to do with employment at all. A classic example of this would be a stay-at-home parent who devotes his or her time and energy to raising the family's children and keeping a household, but isn't receiving a paycheck in any traditional sense. That person can work just as hard, and be just as fulfilled, as anyone else without having a "career" that would show up on a resume.

The same could apply to retirees and volunteers. Their careers are harder to define, but are just as important.

Also, some people just aren't going to find a lot of excitement and engagement in their paid labors, either temporarily or in the long term. We aren't all lucky enough to do something that we love for work. That doesn't mean we can't find ways to enjoy it, though, or to get a sense of satisfaction from it.

There's always room to move toward a different career path, or to get from one position that you don't enjoy to another one that's a better fit for your talents and temperament. But if your so-called "dream job" is beyond what you can realistically accomplish with your talents and/or qualifications, there is nothing wrong with doing honest work that supports you. And it helps if you can see a tie between your inputs and a bigger goal.

The classic example of this is the story of the three bricklayers. The first says he's working for a paycheck. The second wants to earn a wage to feed his family, and the third gets fulfillment because he's helping to construct a church that will bring people closer to God. In reality, we can all represent those three people in just about any job; it's largely a matter of perspective.

Another reason to separate career from purpose is that a lot of people know and find their best use but fulfill it in a non-employment role. For instance, someone who drives a city bus during the day may not feel completely enthralled by what they do for money but gets a little bit of satisfaction from knowing they are helping people travel safely in an efficient and inexpensive way. At night, they could volunteer as a tutor for children in a homeless shelter and fulfill their role as a teacher and mentor, giving a fresh start to young people who haven't been fortunate.

We tend to sell ourselves short when it comes to understanding our own talents and capabilities. Throughout history there have been people – like Joseph, who was sold into slavery, or Mother Teresa who started out as an "ordinary" nun – who are able to accomplish great things because they followed their faith, gifts, and passions. You don't know where your talents could take you or what God has in store for you. If you're willing to trust him, though, he may lead you on an extraordinary path that you could have never imagined for yourself.

It's also important to remember that you can't see the whole picture the way the Lord does. You simply don't know how your contributions affect others and his plan for the universe. A CEO can be successful in creating a company that allows his employees to work, make money, and support God's kingdom with their contributions or free time. A doctor could save someone who will be instrumental as a missionary later. A restaurant server might improve someone's mood and inspire them to create a wave of teaching or giving that goes on for decades.

We are all drawn to certain jobs and roles for a reason. Finding your purpose is about more than earning a paycheck or climbing the career ladder, though, and it's always a good idea to keep that in mind regardless of where you are in life and your work.

Purpose Is About Innate Talents

When thinking about your purpose, place more emphasis on your innate talents than the items on your resume. For instance, even if you have decades of experience as an accountant, if your passion is in creating art, know that this might be your real calling.

Does that mean you necessarily have to quit your day job immediately and take up painting as a full-time occupation? Of course not, but it *could* suggest that the Lord could use your artistic gifts as much as your skill with a spreadsheet. Or it could suggest you have a capacity to help grow God's kingdom in a number of different ways. Becoming a missionary and moving to India can be a fantastic way to spread lights in this world. Finding a way to fund a thousand preachers who spread God's word overseas is obviously equally powerful in a different way.

To know which path is for you, you have to understand your innate talents.

A great many people find themselves shoehorned into careers that aren't much of a fit for their talents, dreams, and personality traits, often because they made decisions that seemed easy or logical near the beginnings of their careers. This can lead to a sense of long-term frustration and under-achievement.

Remedying the situation is sometimes as simple as finding a new outlet or can involve a complete overhaul of someone's life and career. We'll talk about the best way to evaluate these kinds of options through prayer and consultation later, but for the moment what's important is that you're honest with yourself about where your real talents are. They don't necessarily have to match the items in your education, training, or professional experience; they just have to represent the qualities that make you uniquely great at one kind of skill or activity.

By the same token, your purpose should be driven by an honest evaluation, not your wishes. While you might dream of being a great entertainer or someone who is a natural leader, those notions aren't going to help you much if you are highly introverted and tend toward being a logical organizer.

It's not unusual for people to feel pressure to be something they aren't, or even to want to be something they aren't, in our society that prioritizes the spotlight and diminishes the accomplishments of those who work behind the scenes. As long as your purpose and talents are honest and authentic, in every sense of the word, they are going to be right for you.

Also note that God may well have placed us in a "day job" not for our own enjoyment, but because he wants us to touch and influence the lives of others. From our earthly vantage, that's an easy detail to miss. Our own challenge is to ask ourselves what God is seeing and how our perspective on the situation or opportunity might be different if we try to look through his eyes.

It's no good to excel at something you can't stand or to set your sights on a role that isn't a good fit for your talents. Do not be tempted to try to put yourself into a role where you don't fit or to be something that you really aren't. By giving into the urge to draw away from what God wants you to be, you're being kept from your true role in the kingdom. That's being wasteful of your gifts and is a recipe for frustration.

Finding Your Purpose

As was the case with values, your purpose might not be as obvious or apparent as you expect. Certainly, you'll probably have some sense of what kinds of work and challenges you enjoy, but these don't necessarily transfer directly into jobs, tasks, or roles you can fill.

Brainstorming and journaling is again a good place to start, since memories and impressions can be powerful guides. You'll want to be sure you get past the basics, though, and into the reasons behind your preferences.

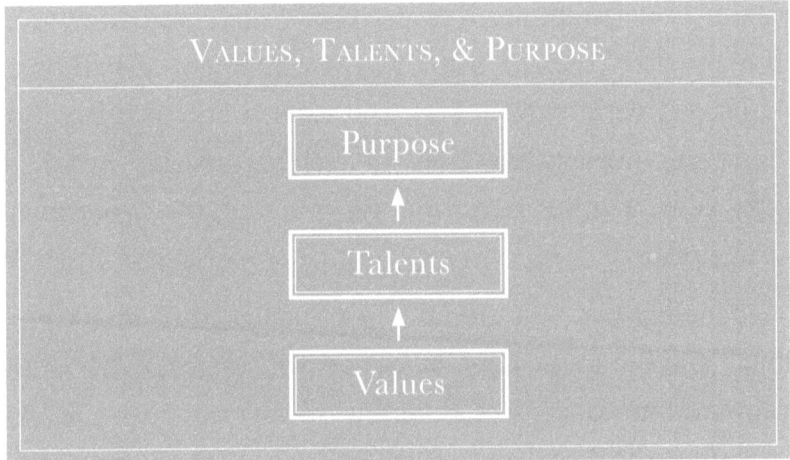

For example, suppose you recall that you had a lot of fun organizing a project in school. What made that experience so special for you? Was it taking on a position of responsibility, outlining the steps so they could be followed later, or maybe getting the chance to pass on what you already knew to someone else?

There can be a tendency to look for quick answers here when nuance and thoughtfulness are the key. There are slight differences between teachers and mentors, leaders and supervisors, or planners and organizers. The better you can understand yourself, your talents, and the things that give you joy, the more easily you can find the places where your purpose fits with the work of others and in God's plan.

As I've already mentioned, other people can sometimes be a great help in discovering your purpose. That's because they may notice things that you don't, such as abilities you didn't realize you had or the way you go into a certain type of project with extra energy and excitement. You have to trust your own instincts, of course, but another person's perspective can be even more enlightening than your own in this regard.

Mentors can be especially helpful, since they don't just know you but know how the talents you have can probably translate into dozens of different roles. They have the life experience to help you understand where you are, where you're going, and how you fit into different projects and organizations. In that way, they can certainly help point you in the right direction, but also steer you away from frustrating mistakes you might not have otherwise noticed.

An additional way to get new perspectives on your purpose is by undergoing personality tests and aptitude evaluations. While these used to be almost exclusively for executives and big corporations, the Internet (and popularity of the test themselves) has made them widespread. So, for a few dollars and less than an hour of your time, you may be able to get a scientific assessment of your talents and disposition.

While these aren't necessarily completely conclusive, they can be good for pointing you in the right direction and getting you to think about qualities you might not have realized you have. That's especially true if you try a few different ones and get consistent results or feedback along the way. Even if you don't consider yourself to be analytical, creative, or introverted (as examples), it may be worth considering the possibilities if those are the kinds of profiles you are assigned time and time again.

You Can Have More Than One Purpose

One difficulty in determining your purpose is that it's not necessarily going to be the case that you have just one. You may in fact be talented in several different areas. That's certainly a blessing, but it can also bring challenges, since you could have a hard time deciding which ideas or possibilities to pursue.

A common answer is to make a rational decision for your career life (that is, to explore the purpose that gives you some mixture of happiness, fulfillment, and financial stability) while leaving room in your personal or private life for other roles you want to fill.

I've already mentioned volunteerism as one such avenue, but there are also opportunities for you to fulfill your purpose, or secondary purpose, at church, within your family or through your hobbies. Some people even turn their talents and interests into second careers, offering them the chance to explore different passions and ambitions at different times.

Some of you may have a gift for teaching and influencing others, for example, making you a natural choice to lead a Sunday school class or Bible study discussion. Others may have a talent for leadership that can best be utilized within coaching. In truth, there are dozens and dozens of talents, and combinations of them, but every one of them has a place and purpose in God's plans.

It's possible your real purpose may change over time. People who throw themselves into a career and then retire, or devote themselves to raising children for a decade or more, will know exactly what I'm talking about. The specific challenge may end, and your role or purpose might shift to something new at the same time.

Note, however, that many of us find that situations change more quickly and readily than our purpose does. Someone who is oriented heavily toward family might find more joy and purpose in raising foster children than they would shifting their attention to a secondary career. Likewise, retirees who leave the business world often find they still have a hunger to lead, manage, and help organizations grow. That kind of drive can serve them well in nonprofits, Christian missions, and second careers.

Your purpose, like your values, is an important part of what makes you unique, but don't confuse what you *do* with who you *are*. God has talents he gives to each of us and a plan for all of our lives. That doesn't necessarily remain constant from one period to the next, though, and a big part of finding happiness is understanding those changes and points of transition.

Your Purpose and Values Are the Keys to Happiness

By now, you probably understand that I don't think it's easy to live in the light without having the foundations I mentioned in the last chapter in place. It would just be too hard to find peace.

But being on the path that God wants for you isn't just about eliminating fear and anxiety – it's also a matter of being engaged and feeling like you're "in love with your life." For that, understanding your values and purpose is absolutely key.

It's no use trying to live a generically "good" life that doesn't suit you. It's like eating someone else's favorite meal. Every one of us is different, and there isn't just a reason for that but consequences as well. Each of us has a responsibility to find the life we were meant to live and discover what God had in store for us when he put us on this earth.

Accordingly, I hope you'll take as much time, reflection, and even input from outside sources as it takes to discover where your passions, talents, and ambitions lie. That's a process that takes years or longer for some people, but having your gifts match your place in the world is one of the easiest ways to find joy.

SEEKING THE WAY

✓ *Which personal values mean the most to you? Why do you think God has given you those and not others?*

✓ *In what ways is your life in alignment with your most important values? In what ways is it not?*

✓ *How well does your career match your purpose and talents?*

✓ *If you know your main purpose, what other purpose might you have? How is your purpose changing over time?*

✓ *How can you use your gifts to better help God's kingdom and find peace in your life?*

CHAPTER SIX

Temptations and Distractions

Consider it pure joy, my brothers and sisters, whenever you face trials of many kinds.

– James 1:2-4

*I*n a perfect world, we would always feel close to God, and like we were fulfilling his purpose and serving one another each and every day.

If that part of our world exists, though, I've never been to it. The reality is that doubts, fear, material concerns, and distractions often get in the way, leaving us to feel as if we are pacing on a treadmill, one day after the next, with only small breaks (like family vacations and spiritual retreats) to look forward to as we climb one hill after another.

In many ways, that's the *opposite* of living in God's light, but it's also indicative of the struggles we face. In a lot of religious texts and seminars, finding God and accepting Jesus is treated almost like an ending point in a person's life. While they may have had troubles before – even serious ones with addiction, crime, or psychological issues – they finally accept God's word and live happily ever after.

I don't necessarily think that's incorrect, but it does potentially give people the wrong idea. Coming to Christ is a new beginning like no other, but it doesn't necessarily signal the end of your earthly concerns or ensure you won't become distracted or misguided in the future. Although it would be great to have no earthly problems or concerns after we accept Christ into our lives, that's simply not going to be the case. Jesus tells us himself to expect troubles.

> *I have told you these things, so that in me you may have peace. In this world you will have trouble. But take heart! I have overcome the world.*
> – John 16:33

For all the new Christians you know, think of how many have strayed from the path. Most of us know men and women who have either stopped believing in God's word or fallen into the trap of living their lives as if they don't.

Often, we think of these people as being pulled into sin or becoming too focused on worldly things. There's probably some truth to that, but another factor is that your faith, just like anything else important in your life, needs to be encouraged, renewed, and recharged.

We should all take that as a warning of what's possible if we don't take threats to our faith, or the life we build in God's light, very seriously.

In this chapter, we're going to look at some of the common distractions, temptations, and challenges believers face while trying to pull themselves onto the path, understand their values and purpose, and find inner peace.

You Can't Walk on the Path If You Don't See It

You make known to me the path of life; you fill me with joy in your presence, with eternal pleasures at your right hand.
— Psalm 16:11

It has been said many, many times that you can't hit a target you aren't aiming for, and that certainly seems to be true in a spiritual sense. In the opening for this book, I mentioned that most Christians have had the sensation, at times, of feeling like their lives were in balance, their faith was strong, and they were content (or at least accepting) of all that was happening in their lives and the world around them.

I also mentioned that most of us don't live in that mental and spiritual space very often and that many believers actually tend to think of that situation as being a happy accident, rather than something to strive for.

If you're one of those people, this book can't help you until you get over that notion. The struggles we face in this world are real, but they aren't all that make up life on earth. Instead, we can have peace, satisfaction, and even love and excitement, but we have to be willing to look for them and embrace them when they're found.

That requires us to rid ourselves of the notion that every moment of life has to involve pain and tests of our faith. It also means we have to lose a certain amount of skepticism if we are holding on to feelings that tell us peace and happiness are "too good to be true." You only have to look at some of the people around you – and within your Scriptures – to see it isn't the truth. God does want us to find a measure of comfort in this life, but he doesn't necessarily grant it to us immediately when we accept him, get baptized, or attend regular church services.

You can't walk on the path if you don't see it, and you can't have peace through your faith if you don't believe that such a thing is possible. In the same way that you believe in God, you have to trust in his gifts if you want to receive them.

It's Easy to Hold Yourself Back

Are you the kind of person who's naturally negative, skeptical, and untrusting? If so, those feelings could be holding you back from happiness.

> *A glad heart makes a cheerful face, but by sorrow of heart the spirit is crushed.*
> — *Proverbs 15:13*

It's easy to think of contentment and peace as qualities that arise from our circumstances. In other words, people have a tendency to think they'd be happy if only they won the lottery, received a big promotion at work, or could enjoy life with the sort of mate and children they've always dreamed of.

In reality, though, earthly success and the right spiritual mindset usually come from an attitude of joy and peace, not the other way around. In fact, it has been shown again and again that negative people who enjoy a bit of good fortune will almost always end up being unhappy again in a very short amount of time.

The opposite is true of those who actively look for the bright side of things. Even though a major loss or setback might throw them into despair for a while, they tend to "bounce back" remarkably quickly.

This isn't just an interesting bit of philosophy, but a way of showing something we all intuitively know and understand. Negative thoughts – whether they revolve around jealousy, envy, worry, or uncertainty about the future – tend to multiply and grow within us. They turn into confusion, doubt, and temptation when we let them fester.

Concentrating on our faith, and what's good, has the opposite effect. It frees us from those mental chains and lifts us up in a way that's enlightening and fulfilling all at once.

Our world is one where everyone seems to be in a questioning frame of mind at all times. While a small bit of skepticism can be good when dealing with strangers or evaluating business situations, holding on to too much of it does more harm than good. We can even start to question God and his word, along with seeing the worst in others and assuming they have bad intentions for us.

Put together, these feelings and emotions weigh us down, stopping us from feeling free and walking in God's light. Don't let too much negativity hold you back from the life you could be living and the peace you could be enjoying. Such feelings aren't ever going to help you, but they may take a heavy toll on your health and spirit over time.

The Burden of Bad Habits and Sin

Although negativity is its own kind of bad habit, and a powerful one, it's worth saying a few words about actual

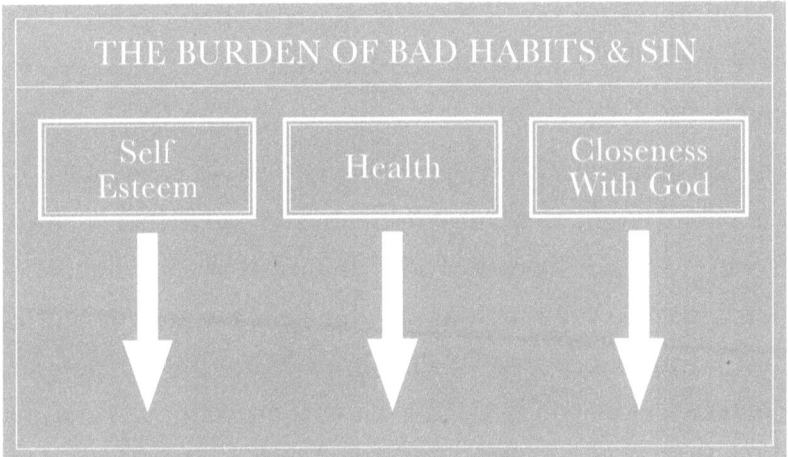

behaviors, too. Bad habits are something we all have and live with, to a degree, but recognizing them and cutting back on the worst can be a good way to bring yourself closer to your path.

Why? There are a few reasons. First, our worst habits are usually bad for our health. Poor health means lower energy, less mental clarity, and a difficult time keeping our thoughts straight. We can't appreciate all the gifts and blessings in our life when we're constantly feeling under the weather, and much of that can be traced to the way we eat, sleep, and generally behave.

Bad habits also have a way of wearing down our own self-esteem. Usually, when we have bad habits we can't get rid of, we start to associate a little bit of shame with them, feeling like we should be strong enough to overcome them, or at least more committed to moving in the right direction. Once our self-worth starts to be degraded, it's easy for other bad habits, and even more serious sins, to creep into the picture.

And finally, as you've probably noticed in your own life, many bad habits either *are* sins or tend to lead to them (which is why we label them as "bad" habits in the first place). I don't have to say much about this because the concept is fairly straightforward. When we are buried under sin, we don't feel close to God. And the farther we move from his light, the harder it is to enjoy peace and comfort.

We're going to address the topic of changing habits and moving toward your path thoroughly in the coming chapter, but know for now that doing things you know you shouldn't is never a good way to bring yourself closer to either God or happiness. Take note of the bad habits you have, record thoughts about them in your journal or workbook, and start thinking about ways you can replace them with better activities in the future.

Taking a bit of time to face up to them, and think about how they could be conquered, might save you a bit of effort and strife later on in this process.

The 3 P's to Overcoming Material World Distractions

Contrary to what a lot of people would have you believe, it's very difficult to find inner peace through Christ when you're

**PRAY
PEOPLE
PLAN**

struggling with problems that have to do with the material world. Financial difficulties, health issues, and career worries are just a few of the distractions that can make it hard for you to feel calm, relaxed, and focused on your faith.

But that doesn't mean it's impossible to walk on the path when you're dealing with earthly concerns. In fact, those are the times when it's most important for you to be in God's light, since your faith can ground you through a tough time and help you make better decisions.

There are really three good methods of overcoming challenges of the material world.

The first is to simply make a plan and start taking action. A lot of our deepest worries and fears tend to evaporate once we decide on a course of action. In other words, when we know what we're going to do about a problem, it seems a lot less pressing. More sleepless nights have been caused by worry about the unknown than they ever have about a defined issue or challenge.

Whatever kind of struggle you're facing, learn more about it (including your options for moving forward), and then just get started. Facing the problem head-on and deciding to do something will make your thoughts more positive and pull you toward the path, almost immediately in most cases.

As we discussed earlier in the book, God has wired us to solve problems. So we need to get to the facts of a situation as soon as possible to avoid dwelling on the negative and becoming emotionally overwhelmed. With the facts, we can face the problem as it truly is and start working on solutions.

Another good step is to find someone who can help you. This can be a friend, family member, or spiritual advisor; it could also be someone from outside your normal life who has specific expertise (like a doctor or lawyer, for example). This is something we'll address more fully in the next chapter, but seeking out help is really just another way of making a plan and taking action. Doing so is almost bound to make you feel better because it leads to less uncertainty and more understanding.

The third thing you can do is simply stop worrying and turn the issue over to God, asking for his peace and guidance along the way. For some problems, this isn't just the best answer but the only one. There are always going to be challenges we can't resolve on our own without his help, and certainly not in a short amount of time. That means we have to learn to live with them, or at least get past them spiritually, which is where prayer and reflection come in.

God never gives you a challenge you can't handle, and learning to put your faith in him for the right outcome, regardless of whether it's the outcome you want or not, is a good exercise that can bring you closer to the path.

No temptation has overtaken you except what is common to mankind. And God is faithful; he will not let you be tempted beyond what you can bear. But when you are tempted, he will also provide a way out so you can endure it.
— *1 Corinthians 10:13*

With that being said, however, the best course of action for dealing with earthly problems that have you preoccupied is usually an approach that combines all three steps. That is, research the issue and take action while seeking the help of an expert, but ultimately go to the Father in prayer and leave the outcome to him.

It can be tempting to simply say "the Lord will deal with it," but my experience has been that God likes us to act on our own behalf when we can.

My feeling is that God wants us to trust in him and his plan, but not to use that as an excuse to avoid leveraging the talents he has given us.

Worldly problems can seem pressing and overwhelming, even for the most faithful. But by combining faith with action, we can overcome these distractions and ease our minds of the worries that keep us away from our path.

> *For we live by faith, not by sight.*
> — *2 Corinthians 5:7*

Facing Up to Serious Problems

Even within the category of "bad habits" and "earthly distractions," there is another topic that needs to be mentioned and addressed: facing up to serious challenges.

In this case, I'm not talking about common money or relationship issues, but difficulties stemming from addictions, instances of past abuse and psychological trauma, or psychological issues that can affect individuals. Each of these can add a unique challenge to the process of stepping into God's light and finding inner peace, of course, but none of them is insurmountable.

If you have a serious issue that's stopping you from exploring your faith, drawing closer to God, or feeling content, the first thing you have to do is decide you're going to tackle the problem head-on. Don't hide from it or ignore issues and symptoms. That might be easier, but it's probably not going to help.

At the same time, don't feel like you have to take on your struggle all by yourself, either. Aside from the numerous therapists, experts, and support groups that are out there, you're likely to find lots of support within your own church or spiritual community. In fact, even if you aren't a member of any congregation, any spiritual leader you meet with will likely be happy to point you in the right direction and toward others who understand your struggle and can put you in touch with the right resources.

There are a lot of different problems that plague us on this earth, but you aren't the first person to have dealt with them and you won't be the last. It certainly is a burden to be tested in this way, but that's not a sign that God has given up on you. In fact, it may be that he has something special planned for your life or that you have an important role in helping others out of the darkness, too.

Consider the utterly *extreme* trials so many biblical figures faced in their lives and the good that ultimately came from them. Take a moment to deeply reflect on feelings about Peter, who was jailed for his faith; Job, who had everything taken from him by Satan; or Jacob, who was forced to leave his home.

What would you feel in their situation? Would you maintain your faith and focus? And if you did, why couldn't your story be similar to theirs?

In life, you can't get to where you're going without being where you've been. And with God's help, you can always get to where you need to be. There isn't anything affecting you so deeply that you can't enjoy a better life and the peace that comes with knowing God and understanding his plan for you. So regardless of what you've been through in the past or what kinds of troubles have come your way, don't let them stop you from moving into the light.

Getting Past Stress, Pain, and Fatigue

Although I included physical problems and issues with physical health under "worldly concerns," the fact of the matter is that stress, pain, and fatigue can all take their toll — not to mention make it harder for you to walk the path that God has laid out for you.

It's a physiological fact that our minds and bodies are interconnected, meaning that few of us can shrug off anything more than minor discomfort without having it affect our thoughts and emotions in a profound way. When we're in lots of pain, it forces our attention back toward ourselves and away from the spirit.

Also, experiencing pain on a continual basis can make us feel like we are being punished or that God is ignoring our cries for help. That's never the case, of course, but it's difficult to see past the layer of physical stress caused by illness or injury.

Even by biblical standards, few suffered like Job did. And yet, he didn't lose his faith – in fact, he's now thought of as an icon of perseverance that believers can draw on when their own hardship and struggles seem too severe. Pain can be obscuring, and even blinding. But physical hurts and limitations don't last forever – God's love does.

It's important to note that a lot of physical problems are self-inflicted. That isn't necessarily to say that you are to blame for your issues, but a recognition that medical professionals readily admit that lifestyle factors are incredibly powerful. If we eat poorly, fail to get the right amount of rest, or abuse our bodies with alcohol, drugs, and other foreign substances, we can't be surprised when our energy is low and our thoughts aren't as clear as they could be.

For that reason, changing our habits – and adopting a healthier routine – can be an important step toward pulling closer to God. The Bible advises us to treat our bodies as temples, and that certainly doesn't include neglecting them.

When it comes to chronic problems and illnesses, a different approach is in order. If the issues can't be resolved with regular changes in diet and exercise, for example, then we should seek out those treatments that are beneficial instead of ignoring the problem. Although we may not feel 100%, simply doing what we can may bring us closer to peace.

When it comes to general issues of poor health and recurring challenges (like weight gain or low energy), the continual process of improvement and renewal can be self-sustaining. That is, the more effort we put into growing our faith and leading good lives, the better we feel, and the more healthy habits we adopt as a result. That naturally leads to more good feelings, and the cycle starts all over again.

The same thing happens when we spiral downward, of course, so we should all take care to monitor not just our health, but how it's being impacted by our spiritual selves and other things going on in our lives.

In cases of sickness, or bodily harm caused by accidents, simply deciding to "feel better" may not be enough. In these circumstances, making serious lifestyle changes may not even be possible, or medicine could leave us with side effects that cloud our thinking.

If you find yourself in this kind of situation, know that God is looking out for you and don't be afraid to ask for his help (and the help of others in your church or community). And take solace in the fact that many of us can actually *improve* our spiritual well-being in the midst of physical struggles. That's because the increased stress has a way of stripping away all the minor things that distract us in day-to-day life, leaving us focused on what really matters.

Adopting a More Spiritual Focus

Even when we aren't suffering from physical problems or major crises in our lives, it can be incredibly easy to become so distracted by earthly matters that we lose touch with our spirituality and drift farther and farther from our path.

In our minds, we may know that certain aspects of our career aren't really that important or that we're letting ourselves be tempted by an unimportant hobby or activity, but that doesn't stop things like greed for wealth, or lust for entertainment, from taking up more mental space than they should.

> *But the worries of this life, the deceitfulness of wealth and the desires for other things, come in and choke the word, making it unfruitful.*
> *— Mark 4:19*

When we care too much for worldly things, our spirit suffers, as does our quality of life. Although there are a lot of joys to be found on earth, the very best of them aren't shown in catalogs or television commercials – they are the spiritual gifts we get from the Lord, our friends, the community, and the charitable things we do.

It's somewhat ironic that the more attention we pay to worldly concerns, the worse our life here in the world gets, but that's a reality that has been noted time and time again. Perhaps Apsley Cherry-Garrard, a member of Scott's expedition to Antarctica, summed things up best. After spending months in a barren landscape with the most basic of rations, he noted, "The luxuries of civilization satisfy only the wants which they themselves create."[1]

Luckily, there is a simple answer to this problem, and it goes back to the advice I gave earlier: Cultivate your faith and a strong perspective on a daily basis. Whether it's through devotionals, fellowship, or some other means, work to adopt a more spiritual focus that keeps you grounded. Avoid the temptations that lurk all around us, promising fulfillment but leaving you empty.

The gifts you really want, in this world and the next, can only be found when you lift the veil over this world and see material concerns for what they actually are. Pay too much attention to what's right in front of you, though, and you may miss the best parts of the journey.

Do You Enjoy Your Temptations?

Legend says that the great St. Augustine once cried out in prayer, "Oh Lord, give me chastity... but not yet."

---

1 *The Worst Journey in the World*, 1922

The idea that he wanted the gifts of the spirit, and to be pure of heart, but was too busy enjoying his sins in the present moment is both ironic and all too common. Even though he supposedly uttered those words in the 15th century, they could just as easily apply to many Christians today.

The fact of the matter is that many of us have sins we hold on to simply because we enjoy them. Even though we know they're wrong – or maybe even *because* we know they're wrong – they give us a quick rush, or an instant sense of satisfaction, we are afraid to let go of.

Are there any sins or temptations in your life that fall into this category? Only you know for sure, but don't kid yourself into thinking they are safe, harmless, or easy to get rid of.

The sins we hold on to grow stronger over time, making them into addictions as much as bad habits. We rationalize them to ourselves, and maybe even to others, knowing that they are holding us back from bigger and better things.

One way to rid yourself of sins you're enjoying is to simply admit the problem. Like so many things in life, the issue becomes infinitely easier to tackle once we have actually acknowledged it and understood its parameters. Think about what it is you really enjoy about the sin or temptation, and then what it might say about you if you can't seem to let go.

Another good strategy is to ask yourself where this particular temptation is bound to lead in the future if you don't relinquish it. Are there bigger consequences, on earth or thereafter, if you can't bring yourself into obedience? Will committing this act again and again draw you into doing something worse or make life more difficult for yourself or your family?

And finally, you can simply ask yourself whether the temptation is worth it. The steps I'm outlining in this book, and especially the path of self-discovery, are all about bringing you closer to God and introducing peace, comfort, and contentment into your life at the same time. I can't think of any idea or activity I would cling to before claiming that prize, and you probably can't, either. That in itself might be enough motivation for you to take action and give the temptation up.

Don't let any particular sin or temptation drag you down simply because you don't think you have the strength to face life without it. Your inner peace and happiness ultimately mean more than any bad habit. We've already seen that God won't make us endure more than we can bear. If you have a sin you're particularly tempted with, know that you've been built with the strength to conquer it with God's help.

For an example of a sin that's easy to enjoy, consider the all-too-common shortcoming of overeating. When we overindulge, we aren't just defying God by failing to respect his temple, but we are also making it harder to stay on the path he set forward for us. Why? Because overeating can lead to physical pain, stress, and other temptations – what begins as a momentary failing can become a much larger problem in our lives.

Unfortunately, the addictive nature of many modern foods makes this an incredibly easy sin to commit again and again. Yet, using the tools and ideas described, any of us can overcome it. Once we admit we've been doing something we know we shouldn't have, it becomes easier to face the problem. And certainly, this is one sin that's definitely not worth the consequences.

After we've established those facts in our mind, asking for God's help and avoiding the temptation (like keeping healthier foods around the house, for example) seems a lot easier. What might have seemed like a habit that was too ingrained to break becomes something we no longer need in our lives. Every step off of God's path leads us away from the peace we are seeking.

Distractions Are Just That

No matter how strong a problem or temptation is, know that it's never more than a temporary distraction. God's love is eternal and all-powerful; there isn't anything on this earth that can overcome it.

Inside, you probably know and understand that already. But that doesn't mean you won't ever be affected by a distraction again, and some are certainly stronger and more common than others.

So, rather than simply advising you to take it on faith that you can get through whatever is bothering you and ask you to rely on your willpower, let me just remind you that you have the tools and strength needed to move past them. Things like stress, material worries, physical pain, and persistent doubts can all be thought of as positives if you remember that beating them back is only going to bring you closer to God and make you feel better in the end.

Besides, overcoming challenges in our earthly lives is largely a matter of identifying and understanding them. Once we know what they are, where they live, and how we're feeding them, eliminating them from our lives gets a lot easier.

Although temptations and distractions tend to be largely personal, it shouldn't be lost in this discussion that none of us is alone in the fight. In the next chapter, I'm going to explain how other people – both your inner circle and those you count on to lift you up and help find the way – can bring you closer to the path.

SEEKING THE WAY

✓ *What are your strongest temptations, the ones that seem to come again and again?*

✓ *Which sins and bad habits are getting in the way of your inner peace? How much shame or guilt do you have concerning them?*

✓ *How are stress and fatigue stopping you from adopting a more spiritual focus?*

✓ *Which temptations are you enjoying too much to give up? Why haven't you been willing to part with them to improve your life?*

CHAPTER SEVEN

Relationships and Support

He who walks with the wise grows wise, but a companion of fools suffers harm.

— *Proverbs 13:20*

You've probably already realized by this point that your inner circle – your friends, family, and others you surround yourself with each day – has a big influence on you and your spiritual journey.

So far, we've focused on the relative positivity or negativity they can have on your life. Surrounding yourself with others who share your values and principles can help reinforce them, while being around men and women who aren't living the right way can have the opposite effect.

Beyond the simple "good" or "bad" of their influences, however, it's important to note that there are some kinds of people we specifically need in our lives to be fulfilled and

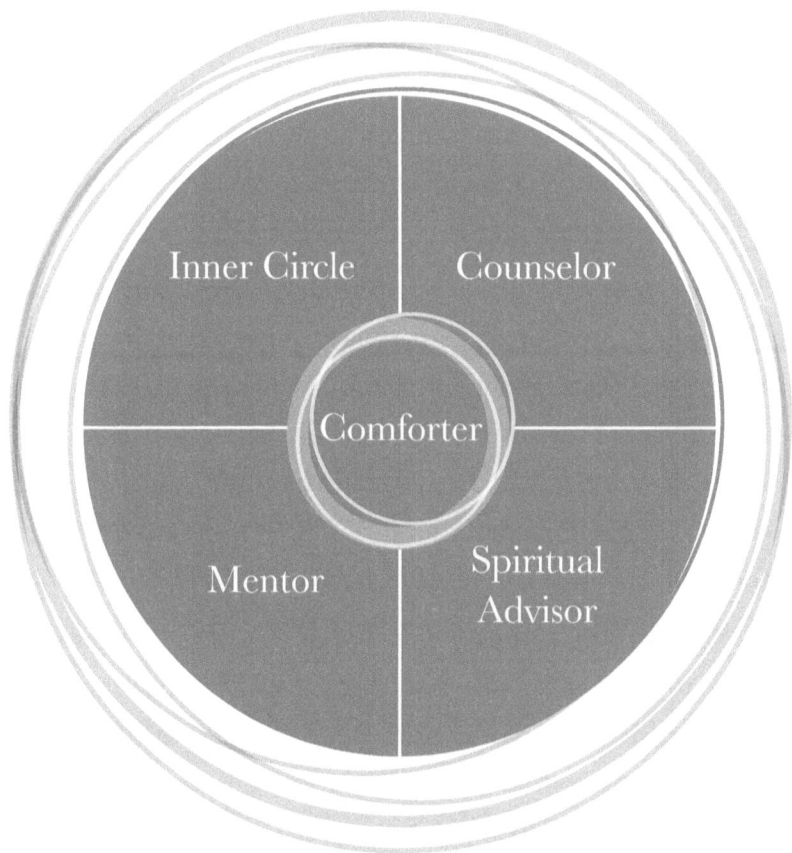

walk on the path. Each of them adds something special and unique, allowing us to grow into the best possible version of ourselves.

In this chapter, I'm going to explain those different roles – which fall into five main categories – and give you a little insight into why each person or group is important. Then, you can better understand and appreciate some of your most important relationships, while also looking to see whether you have important people missing.

Your Inner Circle

Your inner circle can be made up of a group of people. While it's usually composed primarily of your family and friends, and maybe a few coworkers, it could really include anyone you spend significant amounts of time with.

Note that your inner circle doesn't necessarily have to be your family, or at least doesn't have to be limited to them. For various reasons, you may or may not feel close to your biological relatives. Perhaps there is a bit of traumatic history, or you don't share many of the same values. In that case, you can still have an inner circle; it's just up to you to find and form those relationships.

As important as the friends and acquaintances we make in our professional lives are, don't mistake colleagues or "work buddies" for your inner circle. What you need is a group of people that knows you and loves you no matter what – the kind of group you can turn to in times of crisis and need.

The first thing to know about your inner circle is that it's important you have one. In times of stress and joy alike, sharing your experiences and emotions with other people is what makes them special (or tolerable). Without that safety net to fall back on, it's much easier to fall into sin, despair, and depression.

It goes without saying that these relationships don't form overnight, but you can find others to fill your inner circle if you don't have them already. Even if it seems like you're on your own in this world, I can promise you there are others in your church and community who feel the same way. The more of an effort you make to reach out, the more likely you are to find yourself surrounded by men and women who want to integrate you into their lives.

In some cases, you can build your inner circle by adopting a child, becoming closer to a family that you marry into, or even getting involved with civic or charitable causes. In each case, you're going to find other people who either have something in common with you or need to grow their own inner circles, as well.

Another thing to remember is that the relationships you have with the people in your inner circle represent a two-way street. They are there to love, encourage, and support you, of course, but you need to do the same for them. Neglecting your family, especially in the name of material success and other worldly pursuits, isn't just ungodly; it's an almost sure-fire way to end up unhappy and alone.

As iron sharpens iron, so one man sharpens another.
— Proverbs 27:17

The bonds you form and keep with your friends, family, and loved ones are crucial to your well-being. Don't squander them because you're distracted by something that doesn't mean nearly as much. How would you use your inner circle once you have them? That's easy – you'd simply spend time with them.

Family time, fellowship, and social gatherings all make us happier and give us much-needed interaction and perspective in our lives. We are always healthier with them than we would be without them. At the same time, technology and changing social customs have made it easier than ever to become isolated. We can get into contact with just about anyone, but we spend less and less time truly *connecting* with one another.

This has a number of harmful effects on society, of course, but it can also be devastating on a personal and family level. There's something special, and almost magical, about just sitting in a room with your loved ones and doing something together. Through the process of smiling, laughing, and trading stories, we build a closeness that carries through to other parts of our lives.

And, of course, it gives us a chance to tell them what we are thinking about and let them do the same. In this way, the relationships we have with one another are strengthened, and everyone gets the much-needed benefits of having their inner circle together.

Comforter

In many ways, your comforter is likely to be the most important person in your life. Simply put, your comforter's that one person who knows you better than anyone. They are the first person you want to call on the phone when you've had a bad day, and the person you celebrate with when you're proud or overjoyed about an accomplishment.

The fact that *millions* of people currently log on to Internet dating sites every day gives you an idea of just how important these relationships are to us. Most of us, regardless of our age or background, are either extremely fortunate to have found our "other half" or are actively looking for them.

However, while your comforter is often a significant other, I want to be careful to separate romance from the equation, since you don't necessarily *have* to be in love with someone to have them fill this role for you, or vice versa. A best friend or a sibling can sometimes be a comforter, too.

Having someone like that to turn to – a person that you know cares for you and is always going to be on your side – is incredibly affirming. They're going to remind you of your best qualities, encourage you in your faith, and stand up for you when you don't have the faith to do it for yourself.

Your comforter is usually the person who shows up with chicken soup when you're ill, doesn't let you get too down or depressed when things aren't going your way, and even gives you a light kick in the pants when you aren't trying as hard as you could be to reach your goals. Although it's not just about making you happy all the time, it *is* about having someone who only wants the best for you in your life.

Because this relationship will likely influence your attitudes, beliefs, and behavior more than any other, it's important that you choose your comforters carefully. Don't mistake physical attraction, simple friendship, or personal charm for qualities like honesty, loyalty, and integrity. Having a comforter who is constantly in personal turmoil, or is questioning his or her faith on a continual basis, is only going to hurt your own sense of peace and your relationship with God. That doesn't necessarily mean you should write off anyone who doesn't have a perfect life, as none is without sin. It does mean you should be careful about the voices and opinions you're absorbing on a daily and hourly basis.

> *A friend loves at all times, and a brother is born for adversity.*
> *— Proverbs 17:17*

You can have more than one comforter in your life, and that's not necessarily a bad thing given how important they are to our mental and spiritual well-being. One thing you notice time and time again about people is that the moment they lose their comforter, regardless of the reason, they almost always tend to look for another. That isn't because the individuals aren't important to them, but because it's just too hard not having someone they can turn to.

As with the others in your inner circle, it's important that you not take your comforter for granted. Just as you need someone to be there for your highs and lows, they probably want to have a fan, a coach, and a cheerleader who is willing to work for them at various points, too.

In fact, it's not unusual to see marriages and friendships disintegrate over time because one person is too centered on themselves to notice that their partner could use a bit of personal attention now and then, as well. No matter how things are going for you in your work, or your personal life, never forget that you are a comforter for another person just as they are for you, and know that you have to be there to support and encourage them regularly.

Counselor

Because none of us can be an expert on all the important areas of our personal and professional life, we need to turn to counselors from time to time. Some we'll want to have ongoing relationships with because they're helpful or because we know we'll need their advice and input regularly through the future. Others we can turn to once, or only occasionally, as dictated by circumstances.

Examples of counselors in your life might be an accountant, a lawyer, or a medical professional. Because they have a level of expertise and experience we don't, they can help us handle problems we wouldn't necessarily want to face on our own.

Why mention these kinds of counselors at all in a book on faith, spirituality, and happiness?

One reason is that these kinds of people can help us alleviate daily material concerns, allowing us to focus our attention back on our faith and purpose. Another reason is that, just as believers sometimes want to rely on their faith when action is needed, many can be tempted to try to deal with situations that call for professional help on their own.

Certainly, prayer and fellowship are important for dealing with any major situation or challenge, but recognize that a bit of advice or wisdom from someone who knows the territory you're facing, and has helped others in the same situation before, can be a huge help, too.

Listen to advice and accept instruction, and in the end you will be wise.
— *Proverbs 19:20*

Very frequently, the counselors in your life will come from relationships you've built with others in your church or community. For instance, your pastor may be able to refer you to a professional specialist within his congregation, giving you an introduction to someone trustworthy who shares your values and faith. Regardless of where you find them, though, take their advice for what it is — incredibly useful, but not necessarily the end word on any given subject.

Beyond that, just remember that counselors can help you navigate life in this world with simple, practical advice. They can help you fill in gaps in your knowledge and understanding, all while easing your mind and even helping you walk your path more easily. None of us can be all-knowing, and seeking counsel is both biblical and wise.

Spiritual Advisor

If you're reading this book, you probably already have a spiritual advisor, or perhaps several, that you meet with and call on regularly. Nevertheless, there are a few things we should say about these important people because it's critical to not just have the right spiritual advisor, but also to know what you can do to get the most from their guidance and counsel.

For most Christians, the spiritual advisor is going to be a pastor or priest, although a deacon, an elder, or anyone else with a strong base of spiritual knowledge can fit this role, too. These men and women may or may not have a formal, academic background of biblical material, but they will have spent long hours of study and contemplation looking for subtext and nuances within the Scriptures. As a result, they tend to know the Bible better than anyone, and how different lessons or passages apply to modern-day life.

However, the Bible can sometimes be open to interpretation, especially when it comes to drawing broad judgments about God's will. Because of that, it's important that we as believers choose our spiritual advisors carefully. We don't want to be continually skeptical of them, but we *do* want to ensure that their views are biblically sound and in alignment with our own. Sadly, there are some people out there claiming to be messengers from Christ who either misinterpret his teachings or deliberately twist them for their own gains.

While your spiritual guide might be the focal point of your regular church services, don't make the mistake of thinking that's their only place in your life. Sermons and classes can be great for enhancing your biblical knowledge and giving you a weekly reminder of different parts of Scripture. A true spiritual leader knows his or her congregation well.

In other words, you should have a personal relationship with your spiritual advisor and one that includes regular meetings, even if they aren't formal. You can certainly see your priest or pastor in their office, but you could also invite them over for dinner, meet them at a restaurant, or engage them in some other social setting.

This gives you a chance to not only talk about spiritual issues one-on-one, but to let them know what's going on in your life and ask for guidance, perspective, or even just a personal opinion on any challenges you might be facing. Whatever your temptations or shortcomings might be, your spiritual advisor has probably dealt with them dozens of times in the past and may have a few handy resources or Bible verses to share that can help guide you along your path.

Additionally, the spiritual advisor can perform rituals, like weddings or funerals, at important points in your life. This might seem like a small thing, but major milestones and stressful events can be that much easier when you have a friendly, familiar face to call on instead of a stranger. This is yet another reason to invest time in the relationship you have with your spiritual advisor.

It's difficult to give good advice or comfort to someone you don't know much about, which is why you don't want to be a stranger to your personal advisor. They can't do their job, so to speak, if you're just another face in the crowd. And you're not as likely to be as inspired by your spiritual leader, or learn as much from them, if they are little more than a familiar face or a voice from the pulpit.

Mentor

A mentor, in the context of this book, can either mean someone who helps you to develop professionally or just a friend who assists you in your personal or spiritual growth.

Mentors are different from coaches and counselors in that you're not paying them for their advice on a particular instance or situation, but instead have a two-way relationship that's special because of a particular bit of experience or knowledge they have. For instance, your mentor could be someone who has many decades of experience in your professional field or a person who has thoroughly explored a religious topic you'd like to know more about.

The distinction is important because they're invested in you personally and care about your success. They may or may not have the professional credentials that a counselor would, but they're someone you know will take the time to explain things to you because they're in your corner and want to see you succeed.

A good mentor, regardless of how you're using them, is usually someone who sees a bit of themselves in you (and vice versa). What makes them especially valuable isn't their professional qualifications, but the perspective they have from having been in your shoes in the past, along with possibly having mentored lots of other people just like yourself.

It's one thing to know something and quite another thing to have lived through it firsthand. The resulting knowledge can't be bought; it has to be earned. A good mentor, though, can shorten your learning curve – and help keep you from making big mistakes – by using what they know and have seen.

To get the most out of a mentor, you have to choose them carefully, of course. It's never a good idea to have a mentor that's unsuccessful, bitter, or too preoccupied with their own lives to give you any sort of meaningful insights.

Another good idea is to meet with your mentor regularly. Although you may be busy, and your mentor may be as well, developing a good personal relationship is important to getting the most from their wisdom. That's because you and your mentor may have a lot in common, but they'll have trouble helping you if they don't understand your situation, strengths, and personality. Even the best advice doesn't apply to everyone all the time, and meeting with a mentor once a month, or more often, makes it easier for them to get a sense of your situation and point you in the right direction.

Instruct the wise and they will be wiser still; teach the righteous and they will add to their learning.
— *Proverbs 9:9*

Know that, as helpful as having a mentor can be, you can sometimes get even more from mentoring or guiding another person. They say you never learn as much about any subject or topic as you do when you teach it, and that carries over to a lot of parts of your life. You don't necessarily have to be well known or accomplished to mentor someone, or to be much older than they are. Instead, you just have to have skills, perspective, and experience that they don't.

Sharing a bit of that can be very grounding and humbling, not to mention a great way to expand your inner circle and feel like you're "giving back" to another person. So, as you seek out mentors for the different areas of your life, remember that you can fulfill those roles for other people as well.

Do You Have Missing Relationships?

Looking through the list of the five important relationships I've listed in this chapter, do you sense any that are missing in your life? And if you do, is that something you should be concerned about?

Most of us will, at one time or another, have gaps in our most important relationships. A comforter might fall out of our life, a mentor may move on, or we could decide to try another spiritual advisor. As I've said again and again, change is part of the process of life, and that includes seeing new faces come in and out of our inner circle.

Although transitional periods are to be expected, however, having permanent gaps in any of these areas means we are missing out on important resources for fellowship and spiritual growth. You can think of these main relationship categories as major food groups for your spirit. When you go without any of them for too long, it starts to affect your mental and spiritual health.

An outside perspective is always helpful and important. Frequently, we are unable to accurately pinpoint the true cause or catalyst of our pain and uneasiness. Left to our own judgments, we're likely to make miscues and poor assessments. We need other voices in our lives. Without them, we don't feel as grounded and connected as we'd like to, and that opens the door for temptations and distractions.

Even worse, going without an important relationship can put a strain on the others, as well, as you try to put too much pressure onto other existing relationships. Even though some people may fill more than one role in your life, no single person – or even small handful of people – should ever make up the entirety of your social circle. Not only is that too much to ask of any individual, but it limits the number of perspectives you can get on an important challenge or dilemma.

It would be a very rare thing for someone to have their comforter and mentor be the same individual, for example, just as it's usually wise to separate your spiritual leader from a counselor role. They can give insight and opinions, but you don't want to be overly reliant on another person's point of view, or for every event in *their* life to feel like a major event in *your* life.

It may seem odd to seek out others to fill specific roles, especially if they are more social than professional (like a comforter), but realize this isn't as unusual as you might think. If you're looking for someone to be friends with and get close to, there are probably thousands of people living near you who want and need the same thing in their lives.

You don't necessarily have to be formal in the way you think about your friends, contacts, and loved ones or in the ways you approach people to fill different roles in your life. You should make a concentrated effort to ensure you have the relationships you need, though, given that they can be such an important source of comfort and strength.

Trusting God Over Men

All meaningful human relationships require trust, but some of the relationships listed – like the counselor, spiritual leader, and mentor roles – implicitly suggest a level of confidence in someone else's thinking and integrity. In other words, it goes without saying that you have to think highly of someone who's going to supervise your finances, give you advice on your career, or provide you with spiritual training.

Understanding that requires us to be diligent in making the right choices – and also in thinking objectively about those relationships from time to time. That means you don't necessarily want to choose the first person who comes along or to take a blind recommendation from someone else. You have to do your homework to ensure that someone has the right qualifications to help you and that their values are in line with your own.

It *also* means you should never go against your own sense of what is right and wrong, or God's word, on someone else's advice just because you admire their worldly credentials. Ultimately, you're responsible for your own actions and decisions; others can give you advice, but they can't force your hand when it comes to doing something that feels wrong or uncomfortable.

> *Do not conform to the pattern of this world, but be transformed by the renewing of your mind. Then you will be able to test and approve what God's will is— his good, pleasing and perfect will.*
> *— Romans 12:2*

Luckily, these kinds of situations tend to be rare for most of us. But they do happen. You may come into a situation where your lawyer, for example, or even your pastor, takes you down a path you don't agree with or feel uncertain about. In those circumstances, remember that things like degrees and certifications are given by people to other people. God's word is still final and the ultimate resource.

If you feel pulled in more than one direction, my advice would be to pray earnestly on the decision. Remember the advice given to us by Mother Teresa: Don't pray for what you want, but for God's will to show itself. Don't be afraid to dig into Scripture to see if you can find a Bible verse that can help or to seek out alternate opinions from other counselors, mentors, or advisors.

In my experience, taking these steps, with the mindset of discovering what the Lord's plan for you is, is enough to resolve almost any dilemma, ethical or otherwise. It's the process I use for the difficult decisions in my life, whether they're centered on business, spiritual matters, or issues to do with my marriage and family.

Although God gives us others to rely on when we need them, he also gives us the intuition to understand when we are straying from his plan. Trust God over men, and you'll always be on the path to wisdom and contentment.

LIFTING UP OR DRAGGING DOWN?

Usually, when we think of relationships as being "good" or "bad," it's in the sense of whether or not we have a healthy two-way flow of communication. That's important, but as believers we also need to evaluate how healthy our connections with others are in a spiritual sense. Are we spending time with men and women who lift us up closer to God or people who drag us down into temptation?

This can be an incredibly difficult issue to confront. After all, our loved ones are just that: *loved*. We don't want to admit to ourselves or others that they may be a bad influence on us because that would, in turn, require us to take actions that might be uncomfortable. Even if we don't approve of everything they do, we may want these people in our lives. In fact, they may fill one or more of the roles that are so important to our well-being.

I'm going to this topic again in the next chapter, because ending or changing relationships falls under a bigger category of making life changes. For the moment, though, I'd like to point out a couple of things.

First, you shouldn't expect everyone in your life to be perfect, or to live up to an unrealistic standard that none of us would meet. We all have our sins and shortcomings, and we can struggle with the process of overcoming them. You can "love the sinner but not the sin," as the saying goes, especially if you're aware of the challenge it creates.

Just as facing up to a sin makes it easier to resist temptation, knowing that there are harmful aspects of an important relationship makes it easier to change them. Try to be a positive influence in that person's life without being pulled into old habits or temptations, if possible, and see if the relationship can take on a new course.

Another thing to remember is that these interactions function as a two-way street. Sometimes, others pull us into temptation, or activities we know we shouldn't be participating in, because we invite them (either consciously or unconsciously). In that way, you could be a bad influence on someone else. It might be the case that they're trying to get closer to God, and their path, but the habits they have with you are holding them back.

Relationships are complicated, and very often we fall into their different patterns without fully realizing what we're doing. By devoting some conscious thought to the influence you have on other people, and that they in turn have on you, you can begin to turn the troublesome connections you have in your life into something more positive.

And if you can't? That's something we'll tackle in the next chapter.

Letting Others Help Us Walk the Path

Relationships with others factor heavily into our health, our professional progress, and our spiritual well-being. Without the right people in our lives – and the right amount of attention paid to them – we suffer in any different number of ways.

Take some time to think about the people you rely on, as well as the gaps that might be missing within your inner circle, your group of counselors, and the other roles mentioned here. If you aren't getting the help, love, and support you need, now is the perfect time to start making and deepening the connections you have.

It's always easy to think we're too busy to spend more time with other people or that we don't have the knowledge or resources to share what we've learned with others, but those kinds of notions are shortsighted. The fact is, whenever we make others a bigger part of our lives, we don't give anything at all – instead, we find our own lives enhanced.

If you really want to walk the path and live in God's light, you need to be thoughtful about the way you interact with other people and bring them closer. Is your network of relationships and support as strong as it could be?

SEEKING THE WAY

- ✓ *Who is in your inner circle? How are you paying attention to those relationships and keeping them strong and healthy?*

- ✓ *Which person serves as a comforter in your life? How are you serving as a comforter for that person as well?*

- ✓ *Which counselors do you turn to for advice when you need it? Where can you search for others when you require their help?*

- ✓ *How often do you meet with a mentor? How recently have you served as a mentor for someone else?*

- ✓ *What is your personal relationship like with your spiritual advisor? How closely are this person's beliefs and values aligned with your own?*

CHAPTER EIGHT

Finding the Way

For God is not a God of confusion but of peace.
— 1 Corinthians 14:33

*B*now, you've covered quite a bit over the time it has taken you to reach this point in the book. You probably know yourself better than you ever have and have some new ideas about where you fit into God's plans and things you can do to live your life in a more satisfying way.

And, of course, you're probably ready to start walking on the path after all of this study and introspection.

That might not be exactly accurate, though. If you've been following along in your workbook or journal, you've probably noticed something interesting – your life has *already* started getting better.

There's nothing magical or mystical about the reason why; when we think consciously about something, or focus on it, our behavior begins to shift. So just by deciding you want to improve your life and move closer to God's path, you have very likely already done so.

Maybe you've found that certain bits of Scripture inspire you more or that some old sins and temptations don't have as strong a pull as they used to. Perhaps you've been devoting more time and attention to your relationships or thinking about the roles different people could have in your life. It might even be the case that you're more in touch with your own values, and living in a way that's in better alignment with them, because you've seen how important they are to your happiness.

In this chapter we are going to build on that progress and help you to not only continue what you've been doing, but also use what you've learned to step into the light and start to enjoy all the spiritual gifts that come along with it.

Looking Within

Reviewing the notes you've taken during this process, you've probably discovered certain themes or ideas coming up again and again. Some might have to do with areas of your life that you knew needed a bit of change; others could involve previously unrealized values, ideas, and expectations.

Now is the time to put them to work.

What I want you to do is make a list of the conclusions that seem most prevalent or important. Then, instead of using those as a list of complaints or shortcomings, use them to create a vision of your life and future that's more fulfilling. In other words, consider what would have to happen for you to align yourself with your purpose, your values and passions, and the gifts God has given you. Try to find the messages he has been giving you all along.

This isn't just about imagining your "perfect day," although those kinds of exercises could be helpful. What you're really looking for, however, is what it would take for you to feel more complete and satisfied *all the time*. That doesn't mean your troubles and worries would end or that you'd jump out of bed brimming with excitement and joy at the crack of dawn every morning. It just means you would feel balanced, happy, and like you are moving toward the right kinds of goals.

Often, finding the required answers requires a bit of a momentum shift. It's very easy, in our fast-paced world, to get focused on the short term. We all want to know what's going on right now or what's coming up next. When it comes to inner peace and contentment, though, thinking on a longer time horizon – in a span of years and decades – is much more important.

That's because you can't predict what's going to happen, and you're always going to be thrown off the path if you're continually adjusting to one minor issue or another. But, by being intentional with your longer-term targets, you can continue to make progress even when life gets in the way – or if you have to change your goals altogether. When you do, just look out over the horizon to where you want to go and start taking steps.

The biggest dreams we have for ourselves, and the most important parts of God's plans for our lives, usually don't involve small ideas or quick solutions. So we have to give them time to work and stay committed. That's not a bad thing, though, because it makes the feeling of satisfaction we get at the end all the more profound.

STRENGTHENING YOUR FOUNDATION

How would you assess your life based on the criteria for happiness and inner peace I outlined in an earlier chapter? Is your biblical knowledge as strong as it could be? Do you have fulfilling and meaningful personal relationships? Do you know how to manage wealth in a responsible, godly way?

It's nearly impossible to have peace in your life without these pieces in place. They represent the foundation of your path, allowing you to find clarity and live your life free of minor distractions.

It's time to take a look at those notes put together and see which of your foundations may be lacking. Most of us, at some point or another in our lives, find that we are emphasizing one or two priorities, leaving the others neglected or to chance. That's understandable when you think about things from a big-picture perspective, where we are all busier than we'd like to be and may have trouble focusing on our bigger, longer-term goals.

When you have pillars missing from your foundation, it leaves you directionless and out of balance. In fact, whichever part of your life you aren't paying enough attention to now is almost certain to cause you trouble later, meaning that it's going to take even more time and attention to fix.

It's always easier to make time for your spouse than it is to go through a painful divorce. Cutting back to ensure you can pay your bills is far, far easier than filing for bankruptcy. And taking the time to study Scripture to get closer to God takes a small effort in the present but can feel overwhelming when you're looking for specific answers later.

Strengthening your foundation isn't just about finding problem areas, but also thinking ahead to the future. Remember, I told you this chapter isn't just about picking through your lists, but designing the future of your life. Making room for one thing sometimes means turning something else into less of a priority. That's fine and necessary, but be sure you aren't making bad trade-offs by neglecting the pillars of your happiness and contentment.

It's an easy mistake to make, but one that you always end up regretting somewhere down the road.

LIVING WITH VALUES AND PURPOSE

Saying that it's difficult to find happiness without the right foundations in place is somewhat misleading. It's not that the statement itself isn't true – go back and read the last section or the chapter on those foundations again if you doubt it – but it isn't complete.

You won't feel happy and fulfilled without having those bases covered in your life. But meeting those requirements isn't necessarily enough to bring you peace, either.

Never be lacking in zeal, but keep your spiritual fervor, serving the Lord.
– Romans 12:11

That's because of the other part of the equation I already mentioned earlier. In order to truly find contentment and fulfillment, you have to know your purpose and be living your life in a way that's consistent with your values and priorities.

You probably already knew that even before you picked up this book, but there are two problems. The first is that a lot of people never actually take the time to figure out what their values and priorities are in the first place. They don't know what their best skills and attributes are, much less their dreams, preferences, and passions. Hopefully, this book and the accompanying exercises will have helped you with that.

The second and bigger problem is that many people have a nagging sense that they aren't getting what they'd like to be from life, but either ignore those feelings or don't know what to do about them. In essence, they feel trapped by their circumstances, their history, or the expectations others have put on them. This leads them to bottle things up, which is unhealthy for the mind, the body, and the soul.

So don't skip over your personal values and hopes, and don't ignore what you feel. Eventually, keeping your own priorities unexpressed inside is going to lead to bigger spiritual problems and temptations.

And you just might be leaving your very best talents and gifts inside. None of us can know where the future leads, and history is brimming with stories of men and women who had second and third careers, undiscovered talents, and breakthroughs that came from their passions and instincts, rather than their everyday activities. There are artists, writers, painters, architects, and even missionaries who all followed a secret yearning and ended up doing something wonderful and unique.

If you have gifts, talents, and dreams, the Lord has given them to you for a reason. Never forget that you can have more than one purpose and that your purpose can change over time. Find the ones that speak to you now, and then don't be afraid to start taking action on them.

Looking For What's Missing

At this point in the book, one of two things has probably started to happen. Either you've realized you're pretty close to your path, and have a better understanding of what you can do to stay on it, or you've begun to realize you *don't* feel as close to your faith and purpose as you would like.

That's not necessarily the bad news it would seem to be. After all, just by taking the first step of reading through these chapters, and following along in the accompanying self-exploration exercises, you've already moved yourself closer. And, just as importantly, you've probably begun to find labels for the items you feel are missing or deficient in your life.

That means you'll soon be able to create a plan that helps bring you closer.

Regardless of which category you fall into – or if you feel somewhere in between the path and the weeds – I want to challenge you to take some time and consider what might be missing. What are the gaps in your life, your faith, and/or your relationships? What will it take for you to move back onto the path and feel like you're at peace, living out God's purpose for your life?

As you ponder these questions, keep in mind that the answers are rarely singular or basic. Finding peace and contentment is about balance, not just meeting the different items on a checklist. In the same way you might be missing something important, it's entirely possible that you're placing *too much* emphasis on something else that doesn't need to be prioritized so highly.

A classic example of this would be a believer paying more attention to his or her career than family. Finding professional success can make a lot of other goals easier to reach, but it can't replace faith, fellowship, or family. The same is true for the other ingredients to a balanced life. They all matter, but none of them is the *only* thing that matters.

You can't know what to do next, or how to get back on the path, until you realize where important shortcomings are now. Whether you need to make a few small changes or maybe some larger ones that affect several areas of your life, now is the time to start thinking ahead and deciding what you can do to find peace.

As you do, be sure to congratulate yourself for recognizing how and why you need to grow. That's a point a lot of people never come to, and the journey you're on is going to lead you to a destination few ever reach.

Changing Habits

If you do like millions of others each January and pick up a book or magazine article on setting resolutions and breaking bad habits, you'll undoubtedly find lots of cheerful advice and easy-to-use tips. I'm always a proponent of this kind of thing, since it's a great way to learn new skills and keep us motivated for the future.

However, there *is* one thing I think they often get wrong: Breaking bad habits is *really hard*.

It's not that these books necessarily tell you it isn't, but they tend to gloss over the fact that patterns of behavior are deeply ingrained within us. Next to your survival, your brain is hardwired to look for *comfort*. That means doing the same things again and again, even if we don't necessarily enjoy them, because they feel "safe" compared to trying something new.

> *Remember, it is sin to know what you ought to do and then not do it.*
> — *James 4:17*

The net effect is that even when we really, really want to make changes in our lives, we tend to revert back to old ways of doing things.

Luckily, there are methods you can use to trick yourself into changing mindsets, behaviors, and even long-standing habits. One trick is to remember that small things, even *very* small things, tend to add up. Wake up to exercise for 15 minutes every morning, without changing anything else in your life, and you're likely to start losing a pound or so every month. That might not seem like a lot, but over the course of a couple of years, it can make a huge difference in your physical health.

The same principles apply to saving money, reading Scripture, or picking up a new hobby. Just an hour a week turns into 50 over the course of the year, more than enough time to learn a new skill, plan a new activity, or develop a new mindset.

Best of all, making small changes is easier than making big ones, so we're more likely to follow through with them and create new habits that will sustain us going forward. If you want to do something different with your life than you've done in the past, you have to start doing new things. Part of that will undoubtedly mean finding the motivation to study new ideas and try new activities. Another part that's mentioned less often is that you'll have to get rid of your older bad habits to make room for the new ones. You have to let them go if you want to make space for something new.

There are probably a lot of items standing out on your worksheet that you're ready to get started with today. That's wonderful, and I know you're going to do great things with them. But instead of trying to change your whole life around in one fell swoop, why not pick two or three habits you can stick with for the next couple of months? After they are ingrained, you can pick up two or three more, and so on, until you're walking on the path God has set out for you.

It's hard to see, from our limited, short-term human perspective, but very small changes can lead to very big effects, if we will only let them. We know this applies to faith, as well, as given in the Gospels.

> *He replied, "Because you have so little faith. Truly I tell you, if you have faith as small as a mustard seed, you can say to this mountain, 'Move from here to there,' and it will move. Nothing will be impossible for you."*
>
> *– Matthew 17:20*

Making Bigger Life Changes

Although I think everything in the last section is wonderful advice, I'll be the first to admit it doesn't *always* apply. There are some situations that are just so dire, urgent, or overwhelming that major life changes are needed.

Usually, this has to do with past mistakes that have mushroomed into circumstances that are too serious for incremental improvement. As examples, believers who have developed substance abuse problems, fallen into extramarital affairs, or questioned themselves nearly completely out of their faith may find themselves realizing that changing minor habits isn't going to do the trick.

Or you might have the feeling that your life is so far out of alignment with your values and the foundations of happiness we've discussed that you can't see any way back from where you are now.

Regardless of the situation, my advice would be to turn back to the exercises that have gotten you this far into the book. Perhaps your problem is so big and obvious that it overshadows all the others and all the immediate answers point to resolving it. If that's the case, your first step probably isn't to make a "clean break" with your old life; instead, speak things over with a mentor, counselor, or spiritual advisor to find out what a good next step might be.

The farther we are off the path and into the weeds, the more difficult it is to tell what we need to do to get back on track. But abruptly changing career paths, ending marriages, and making other huge life decisions doesn't always work out the way we hope it will. Having another person who can foresee what might happen, and which best steps are available to you, can prevent you from turning a bad situation into a worse one.

It may actually turn out that undergoing huge changes is exactly what you need. Even if that's the case, though, you're going to want others by your side who can support you along the way and remind you why you've made the decisions you have. In other words, they can help stop you from backsliding into sin, temptation, and misery because they'll understand where you have come from.

For most people, a series of small and successive changes in their habits is going to be enough to put them back on the path and allow them to feel the calm and inner peace they crave. But if you're one of the exceptions to the rule, don't try to make huge changes alone when you don't have to – think things through and then get the advice you need to move forward and back into the light.

Recovering From Major Setbacks

As I hope you understand by now, walking the path God set out for you doesn't necessarily mean you're going to live every day in bliss. Although you will feel significantly better much of the time and will probably enjoy happiness, contentment, and other euphoric feelings more often, there are always going to be bad days and minor irritations to make things more difficult.

A special word needs to be said, however, about the really big life setbacks we all suffer occasionally. These can take a lot of different forms, but usually look something like divorce, financial ruin, or a death in the family.

When these kinds of setbacks arrive in our lives, it can feel like the peace we've worked so hard to achieve can go straight out the window. It's natural to wonder what you've done wrong to deserve for these things to happen to you or why God has abandoned you when everything was seemingly going so well.

That's not accurate, of course. The fact of the matter is that big setbacks are part of our earthly lives, and no amount of faith, biblical knowledge, or fellowship is going to stop us from experiencing them. But the closer we are to our path, the more equipped we are to deal with these troubles, and the faster we'll return to our faith and happiness.

Nothing I can write will make the shock of unexpected tragedies and setbacks seem like easy sailing. But I can tell you that turning to the Lord, your spiritual advisor, and those in your inner circle is a good first step. They know and love you, of course, and also might not be so close to the situation. Because their loss isn't as strong, they'll be able to see the setback for what it is and offer you better perspective on what's happening.

> *I can do all things through him who gives me strength.*
> *— Philippians 4:13*

Beyond that, just give yourself the time to work through the issue and be strong in your faith. As I've noted before with illness, it isn't unusual for personal tragedies to actually pull us more strongly into a relationship with God, not to mention those around us. It's only when the bonds are tested that we fully understand just how strong they've always been.

And then, as time passes, return to *Seeking the Way* and go through the exercises again. In some cases, your answers and insights may have changed. More often than not, though, you'll probably find that what you most needed was for the wound to heal a bit and that it won't take you as long as you might have envisioned to get back to where you were on the path before, or to find a new way forward.

Finding Ways to Let Go

We often talk about "finding" peace, but I think that's a little bit of a misnomer. After all, it's not something you stumble into, at least not for very long. Instead, you have to follow a two-step process: First, you set the conditions for peace by arranging your life in a way that's in alignment with your purpose and biblical principles, and then you decide to let go of control.

Nothing you've read in this book, and none of the ideas you've put to use, will matter unless you can take this second step. Reaching for inner peace is a decision; it requires you to accept that there is so much you don't know, can't see, and won't ever be able to control.

That's a simple and obvious idea, but it runs contrary to the kinds of feelings that are so pervasive in our society today. No matter where you turn, someone is offering you more information, more flexibility, and more control – or at least the illusion of control. The reality of life, however, is that we can only control our own thoughts and actions. We should ask God to guide us in those, and then let go of the expectations we have for anything after that.

Letting go isn't as simple as deciding you just don't care anymore – that's indifference, not contentment – but it does still take a conscious effort. That's because no matter where you turn, there are going to be tests and distractions that try to take away your peace. You'll probably never be able to tune them out completely, but you can learn not to dwell on them by turning things over to God.

Toward that end, I would encourage you to replace your anxiety with prayer. Instead of dwelling on things that are wrong or things that might go wrong, immerse yourself in Scripture and surround yourself with others who trust God, and let their contentment rub off on you. Over time, with lots of practice, you'll learn that God's will is always done. It might not be what you wanted or expected, but it's always going to be the right outcome in the long run.

That's where real contentment comes from, and it gives you the ability to stay cheerful, optimistic, and filled with faith in the face of any challenge or obstacle. When you truly believe that the Lord is on your side, loves you, and has a plan for your life in this world, there isn't anything that can take that feeling away or pull you off your path.

Make no mistake: Learning to let go isn't easy, and it takes a bit of practice. It's necessary if you want to live in God's light, however, and it's also the one thing that can keep you grounded no matter what the world has ready to throw at you.

Maintaining Your Focus

Ironically enough, one of the biggest threats to your sense of peace can be your own sense of inner peace.

That probably seems confusing, but it's still true. Although it's easier to remain calm and content once you are already feeling that way, it's also true that we can become too complacent, in our lives and in our faith, to see temptations and distractions for what they are.

I've spent a lot of time on habits in this book, and for good reason. A lot of the work it takes to get onto God's path for you is really just a matter of making small changes to the way you think and act. Over time, these add up to bigger shifts in your life and lead you to where you want to go.

It's just as important to keep those habits up after you've found a sense of inner peace, or all the effort you put into getting on God's path for you can be wasted in a relatively short amount of time. Let little distractions creep in, fall prey to a few temptations, or stop paying attention to God's word, and it's only a matter of time before you start to feel disoriented.

At that point, you'll wonder what went wrong and why you suddenly feel off-balance. The reality is that you simply stopped following God's plan, and then drifted farther and farther from the positive changes you'd made.

Think about it this way: Every move you make away from the path, or every turn you don't take, takes you a couple of steps away from the place where you're happiest and most fulfilled. Put just a few missteps together, and you could be facing the wrong direction altogether, with each step taking you farther and farther from the light. Without even noticing it, you could get to a point where you can't even see where the path has gone and need to backtrack or retrace your steps just to figure out how you got lost.

When you consider how easy it is to take those missteps and be focused on worldly concerns that ultimately aren't as important, it's no surprise that most of us drift in and out of God's light on our own even without a plan. Sticking to your plan and purpose takes lots of small adjustments.

Blessed is the one who perseveres under trial because, having stood the test, that person will receive the crown of life that the Lord has promised to those who love him.

– James 1:12

Your life is going to change. Relationships are going to begin and end, distractions are going to fade in and out of your focus, and different goals, temptations, and opportunities are going to present themselves. The path you should be on today might not look the same in a few months, much less a few years.

For that reason, I invite you to visit this book again in the near future. Read through it once or twice a year, when you have some time to yourself, and try to complete the exercises as if you are doing them for the first time, or at least without holding on to a preconceived notion of what your answers need to be.

Doing that, along with a devotion to reading Scripture and surrounding yourself with other believers, is a good way to maintain your focus in a fast-paced world that's filled with messages that are contrary to God's word. It's not easy to keep your eyes and feet on the path, but with a little bit of conscious effort, you can certainly do it.

Renewing Your Faith and Peace

There are two things you can always expect to encounter in your life on earth, no matter how many years you live: signs of God's love and the continual process of change.

That's important to remember, because being in the light and on the path isn't a singular condition. Sometimes you're there, sometimes you are close, and sometimes you are farther away than you'd like. But no matter how good or bad you're feeling in the moment, tomorrow is a new day and a different challenge is always around the corner.

What I'm trying to suggest to you is that you never relax, get too comfortable, or give up the fight for the peace you want and deserve. Regardless of where you're at today, you aren't going to be promised contentment tomorrow, but it won't be out of your reach, either.

I myself go through the steps outlined in this book at least once every couple of years. Time and time again I've been surprised to find the things I thought I knew and understood about myself have changed or that my position on God's path has shifted subtly and I'm now looking at new goals, challenges, or values I didn't expect or consciously realize.

That sense of constant adjustment might be difficult, but it also shouldn't be surprising. We all age, grow, and adapt. Our relationship with God, ourselves, and everyone around us evolves naturally as a result.

God's faith and peace are infinite, but they take a bit of work on your part. He's willing to give you everything you need to enjoy your life in this world and more, but you have to be willing to work for it and find the right answers – not just once, but again and again.

You're nearing the end of this book, but are still on the beginning of a long journey – a journey you'll make again and again as your life changes and new answers are required. It might be exhausting each time, and you never know where the road will lead, but life is so much better when you're on the path.

SEEKING THE WAY

✓ *How confident do you feel that you have the foundations in place for a fulfilling life?*

✓ *How thorough have you been in identifying your values and purpose? How can you live in a way that makes the most of them?*

✓ *What is something important missing from your life? What will be the first steps to finding it?*

✓ *Which bad habits are most important for you to break? What new habits would you like to replace them with?*

✓ *What major changes in your life do you need to contemplate? Where can you turn to find another perspective?*

✓ *Are you truly ready to trust God and turn control of your life over to him?*

CONCLUSION

Walking the Path

Are you ready to walk on God's path?

In many ways, it would be much easier to simply get swept along by life, moving from one crisis to another, the way so many do. But then we'd be missing out on the very best of what God wants us to have on this earth – the sense of peace and excitement that comes when we finally discover where we "fit" in the puzzle of God's plan.

To me, this is the ultimate journey and the ultimate challenge. It's what makes life worth living, especially when things seem to be at their darkest and lowest points.

I truly hope that, in my own small way, I've been able to help you find the ingredients for a successful and fulfilling life within your faith. This book isn't meant to be an instruction manual, or even a biblical reference. Instead, it's designed to help you uncover your personal roadmap to a happy life.

Like any map, though, it is only helpful to the degree that you actually follow along. Reading and rereading the pages may give you a temporary boost of motivation or inspiration, but only exploring your own talents, values, and ideas is going to yield a better way forward. Likewise, you have to face up to your own sins and shortcomings if you want to put them in the past.

In other words, there isn't an instant cure. God gives us a path to walk on, and the strength to follow it, but it resembles a hiking trail a lot more than an escalator. He'll show us the way, but we still have to shuffle our feet forward, one at a time, if we're going to make any progress. And make no mistake, not all of those steps are going to be comfortable.

I don't know what the future holds for you, but we all experience pain, strife, and turmoil at different points. Walking on God's path doesn't diminish our troubles; it gives us the strength to handle them. It doesn't stop us from noticing or caring when bad things happen; it just gives us the right perspective and the ability to hold on to our faith.

For that to happen, we have to be willing to do the work the Lord has set out for us. That doesn't just mean finding our purpose and fulfilling our role, but undergoing the constant process of renewing our faith and our relationships, continually looking for new ways to find peace and grow his kingdom.

And it means letting go of our false sense of control and turning things over to God. It means asking for his will instead of hoping he'll shift events toward the outcome we secretly desire. That can be a hard adjustment to make, but it's always the right one – our understanding is flawed, but God's plans are always perfect.

Achieving inner peace and a closer relationship with the Lord aren't things that happen by accident. You can make the decision *right now* to start making the kinds of changes that are needed in your life, whatever they might be.

If you haven't found the way forward yet, go back through the self-assessment questions you found sprinkled in these chapters (I've included them in an appendix for easy reference). If you do know what needs to come next, I encourage you to take action immediately. It's very easy to put off tasks that are important but difficult, and it's very easy for "tomorrow" to turn into "someday" or even "never."

The contentment you're looking for is too valuable – and the plan God has for your life is too important – to turn it into an afterthought. The ideas outlined in this book might not be perfect, but they do work. All you have to do is follow them, and then enjoy the multitude of blessings God has been saving for you.

There's nothing as fulfilling as *Seeking the Way*. For Jesus *is* the way. I wish you success on your journey as you are seeking him within your life.

Go in peace. Your journey has the Lord's approval.
– Judges 18:6

Questions to Help You Seek the Way

Throughout this book, I advised you to start a journal, or use the accompanying *Seeking the Way* workbook, to capture your thoughts. You want to have a sense of what your ideal life might look like, along with some ideas of how you can reach it and what kinds of obstacles might be holding you back. If you've already started doing that, you can use this section as a review and a way to see the "big picture" with all the important questions put together in one place.

If you haven't already started journaling, though, take this opportunity to begin *right now*. The most important parts of *Seeking the Way* aren't the ones I've written, but the ones you're going to add as part of your personal journey. This is the most important step you can take. Begin exploring, and you'll find a path to faith and happiness that coincides with your talents and gifts. Skip it, and you'll quickly fall back to a point where you're only on the path for short periods of time.

Remember that your notes don't have to be in the form of a diary or journal. In fact, they don't even have to follow any structure or make grammatical sense. All that's required is that you find a way to sit quietly by yourself, so you can tune out the surrounding world and think deeply about some important concepts and how they apply to you in your life.

In fact, the only rule is that you shouldn't stop until you're finished. If you can find answers you know in your heart to be true within 20 minutes for a specific question, that's fine. If it takes weeks of thought and reflection, with lots of stopping and starting, that's just as good. Eventually, the breakthrough will come. You just have to let it.

Consider the questions you find below to be conversation starters for your brainstorming. They're meant to be broad and to get you thinking. They might not cover everything that matters to you, and not every question will be relevant to your specific life.

Add and expound as needed, and use these as discussion points with those who are close to you. The only thing that matters is you keep working until you get to the truth of God's plan for your life, whatever that might look like.

- ✓ When have you felt most at peace in your life?

- ✓ Can you list two times when you were able to see God working in your life?

- ✓ What are the biggest areas in your life right now where you need to show more trust in God?

- ✓ How often do you prioritize material success over spiritual gifts?

- ✓ How would you explain the difference between belief and faith?

- ✓ Which people in your life show the qualities of living on the path, and why?

- ✓ How do you feel when you're far from God's path?

- ✓ How strongly do you believe finding inner peace is achievable in your life?

- ✓ How personal does your faith feel?

- ✓ Can you think of a few times when you didn't trust God as much as you do other people or secular institutions?

- ✓ What do you currently do on a daily basis to strengthen your faith?

- ✓ Do you surround yourself with other believers in your personal life?

- ✓ How often do you read God's word? What could you do to develop a working knowledge of the Bible?

- ✓ How big of a priority are you making the important relationships in your life?

- ✓ What is your attitude toward wealth? How was wealth or income discussed in your home growing up? What was behind family behaviors and norms?

- ✓ Which sins are particularly troublesome for you? How do they make you feel like you have no power to control them?

- ✓ How strongly do you feel that God has a purpose for your life? How close are you to living your life in a way to serve that purpose?

- ✓ Which personal values mean the most to you? Why do you think God has given you those and not others?

- ✓ In what ways is your life in alignment with your most important values? In what ways is it not?

- ✓ How well does your career match your purpose and talents?

- ✓ If you know your main purpose, what other purpose might you have? How is your purpose changing over time?

- ✓ How can you use your gifts to better help God's kingdom and find peace in your life?

- ✓ What are your strongest temptations, the ones that seem to come again and again?

- ✓ Which sins and bad habits are getting in the way of your inner peace? How much shame or guilt do you have concerning them?

- ✓ How are stress and fatigue stopping you from adopting a more spiritual focus?

- ✓ Which temptations are you enjoying too much to give up? Why haven't you been willing to part with them to improve your life?

- ✓ Who is in your inner circle? How are you paying attention to those relationships and keeping them strong and healthy?

- ✓ Which person serves as a comforter in your life? How are you serving as a comforter for that person as well?

- ✓ Which counselors do you turn to for advice when you need it? Where can you search for others when you require their help?

- ✓ How often do you meet with a mentor? How recently have you served as a mentor for someone else?

- ✓ What is your personal relationship like with your your spiritual advisor? How closely are this person's beliefs and values aligned with your own?

- ✓ How confident do you feel that you have the foundations in place for a fulfilling life?

- ✓ How thorough have you been in identifying your values and purpose? How can you live in a way that makes the most of them?

- ✓ What is something important missing from your life? What will be the first steps to finding it?

- ✓ Which bad habits are most important for you to break? What new habits would you like to replace them with?

- ✓ What major changes in your life do you need to contemplate? Where can you turn to find another perspective?

- ✓ Are you truly ready to trust God and turn control of your life over to him?

About the Author

Tim Crain is a Christian, a keynote speaker, a financial executive, and a US Army veteran. For as long as he can remember, he's been interested in the concepts of success and happiness, and especially how they intertwine with our faith in a confusing world. The biblical answers and insights he's learned along the way can be found in the book you're holding.

Tim has been married for more than two decades and has three wonderful children.

You can find out more about him, including supplemental materials for this book, at www.SeekingTheWay.com.